MITHIAN

IN THE PARISHES OF ST. AGNES AND PERRANZABULOE

By

Tony Mansell

Published by Trelease Publications

First Published July 2003

Published by:
Trelease Publications
The Orchard
Mithian
St. Agnes
Cornwall TR5 0QF

ISBN 0-9545583-0-8

Printed by R. Booth Ltd
Printers & Bookbinders
Antron Hill
Mabe
Penryn
Cornwall TR10 9HH

Contents

Extract of OS map 1907 showing Mithian and the surrounding area

At the time this map was drawn the Great Western Railway (God's Wonderful Railway) line from Chacewater to Newquay had been opened four years. The track through Mithian involved a lot of digging and filling as can be seen from the cuttings and embankments.

The narrow fields to the west of Mithian Farm are thought to be the remnants of a medieval strip field system.

Mithian River (shown as a dotted line) indicates the boundary between the two civil parishes of St. Agnes and Perranzabuloe.

There is evidence of mining activity in fields 1449, 1454 and 3006 but not shown are any uncharted workings from previous times.

The small copse at the north of field 1462 could indicate mining activity or it could be the buried remains of an old building, possibly the lost chapel especially as one of the nearby fields was called Park-an-Eglos.

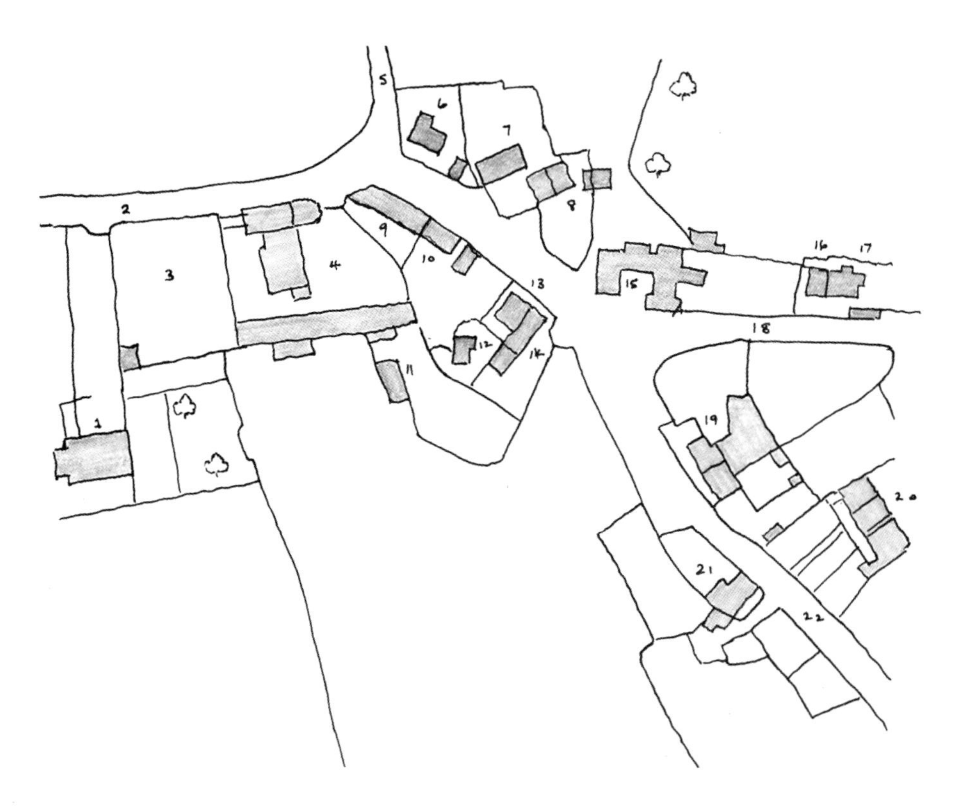

Extract of OS map 1907 enlarged to show village centre

1	Mithian Farm	12	Tuckaway Thatch
2	Mithian Lane	13	Trevene
3	The Mowhay	14	The Olde Forge
4	Mithian Farmyard and Buildings	15	Miners Arms
5	Piggy Lane leading to Trewartha Farm	16	Underwood
6	Mithian Stores	17	Little Willows
7	Sunny Villa	18	The Lane or Brewery Hill
8	Leonora Cottage	19	Mithian Manor Complex
9	Whitewalls Cottages	20	The Terrace
10	Mithian Village Hall	21	The Hermitage
11	Mithian Farm Cottage	22	Chapel Hill

Introduction

Cornwall is my home and I cannot imagine living anywhere other than in a Cornish village. In the world of commerce and industry this may be considered to be limiting but I have never regretted ignoring the advice to move, "up country" and the four years that I spent commuting to Plymouth was sufficient, "foreign" exposure for me. There is an old Cornish saying (well probably Cornish) that, "The further east you travel the more convinced you become that the wise men never came from there."

I have lived in Mithian for over twenty years and my wife, Sue, was born here. Our children are fourth generation attendees at Mithian School and it seemed appropriate that the village should be the subject of my first book.

It is probably fifteen years since I first talked about recording the history of Mithian. Since then, many of the old characters of the village have died and their contribution to this book is sadly missed. I have to accept that this was an opportunity lost and have made considerable efforts to collect as much information as possible from the people who knew them. I guess that is the problem with, "doin things dreckly."

This book has been written to provide a flavour of Mithian past and I hope that you will find it to be interesting and informative. The village is typical of many Cornish communities but the people are unique and their story has never been set in print. Reflecting the tremendous enthusiasm and help given by so many people, a part of any funds left over after the printing and publishing costs will go to village coffers.

The village of Mithian has been described as pretty, picturesque, quaint and peaceful and it is certainly all of these. It has its own charm and the eruption of the furze or gorse as I write makes it even prettier. What other plant has a better claim to be Cornwall's national emblem.

The village has changed very little over the years and holds a special place in the hearts of those who live here or have lived here. More important, however, are the people that make up the community; they are what make it special.

Just as we are interested in who our ancestors were and how they lived, our descendents will wish to know what life was like in the year 2003. The recording of the present day is undertaken in many ways and research will be much easier for future historians. It is surprising, however, the extent to which the past has been recorded or has been the subject of intelligent conjecture. My research has been assisted by those who have gone before and have taken the bother to write things down. A considerable amount of information has been obtained from books, newspapers and other documentation but I have become aware that the written word cannot always be trusted. As one librarian put it, "There are some authors of whom we are a bit wary." Perhaps the old Cornish adage applies, "If tidn true then it oughta be." Other information has been collected by word of mouth and I must express my appreciation to all of those who have sat with me and poured out their memories. I do have a sneaking feeling though that they actually enjoyed the opportunity to reminisce.

Whereas the book is specifically about Mithian it should be considered against the backdrop of events in Cornwall and England. Although there is no evidence of conflicts within the village the various rebellions and wars undoubtedly impacted on the people and there is reference to the national and international conflicts that directly affected families in the Mithian area.

It should also be borne in mind that Cornwall's early history is very different from that of England and that it retained its Celtic language and culture for many centuries after its defeat at the hands of the Anglo Saxons. The Cornish language was still being spoken in central Cornwall during the 1600s and even later in West Cornwall. It was dealt a near fatal blow by Edward VI in 1549 when he refused the translation of the new Prayer Book into Cornish, ensuring that religious services would be in the, "New English." During the English Civil War, or more correctly British Civil War, in the 1640s many of the Cornish soldiers could not speak any English and it is highly likely that they were fighting as much for Cornwall against the new order as for a King who was considered to be extravagant, selfish and out of touch.

Notwithstanding these wider events it is a book about the village of Mithian and. I hope that it will be of interest and that parts of it may even cause a chuckle.

Mithian Village

In, "Cornish Place Names," O J Padel states that Mithian is, *"A completely obscure name, despite the consistent early forms. It looks Cornish rather than English and is clearly an ancient name; but no Cornish, Welsh or Breton word are known that could explain it."*

The Cornwall County Council Monuments Records say that, *"The settlement of Mithian is first recorded in 1201. The name is Cornish, but its true meaning is obscure. The settlement of Mythyanwoeles, Lower Mithian, is recorded only once, in 1341 and the site is lost."*

J E Glover, in his book, "The Place Names of Cornwall," suggests that Mithian is named after a stream containing a derivative of a word related to the Welsh midd, which is an enclosed place or pit, or middi, which is a pit or pool in a river.

There is then, no firm evidence or opinion as to the origin of the name but what of the spelling? Although we now know it as Mithian it has previously been spelt as Mithien, Mydyan, Midhyan, Mithyan, Medyan, Methean and Methyan so you can take your choice. Whatever the spelling, it refers to the hamlet situated about a quarter of a mile inland from the Perranporth/St. Agnes road. It is well signposted and you are very welcome to visit it, hopefully for its own sake and not as a short cut to wherever. As someone once said on emerging from the Miners Arms and in answer to some visitors asking the way, "I'm not sure that you can get there from here."

Mithian is said by some to be the second oldest village in Cornwall and they may well be correct. I do not want to take issue with them but I would be interested to know where that fact came from. There is no mention of Mithian, or of its numerous other spellings, in the Doomsday (Domesday) Book of 1086 whereas there is mention of a number of other small villages such as Callestick, Crantock and Nanskuke. This is not conclusive, however, as many places that are known to have been in existence at that time do not appear in that book. The Doomsday Book records properties rather than settlements; small villages that were part of large estates were ignored. If Mithian did exist at that time then it would have been included as part of another manor - almost certainly Tywarnhayle. One conclusion that can be drawn, however, is that its absence means Mithian Manor had not been established at that time.

St. Agnes and Perranporth were certainly a part of the Manor of Tywarnhayle or Tiwarthel as it is written in the Doomsday Book and, assuming that the village of Mithian existed at that time then it too was a part of this manor. Prior to 1066 Algar held Tywarnhayle but following defeat by the Normans it was re-allocated and the Count of Mortain held it from St. Petrocs. It is described as having 7 h. Land for 20 ploughs; in lordship 4 ploughs; 10 slaves; ½ h. 15 villagers and 16 smallholders with 10 ploughs and 6 ½ h. Woodland, 12 acres; pasture 15 league long and 1 league wide. It pays £14 less 20d. 20 unbroken mares; 10 cattle; 250 sheep. (a league or leaga was 1.5 miles).

The Count of Mortain was a half brother of King William and had holdings in many counties. Tywarnhayle is Chy war an hayl in Cornish and translates into English as, "house on an estuary." I have been unable to determine when Mithian Manor was established but there is later reference to it being occupied by a French nobleman and, whilst I am not suggesting that the Count of Mortain lived here, this person may well have had some connection with him.

Goshen is an area to the south east of the centre of the village and it is possible that its name comes from the bible. The name refers to that place where the Israelites lived when they were held in slavery in Egypt. Jericho valley is nearby and leads down to Trevellas cove and here again the name has a biblical connection.

Mithian, or rather Methean, is mentioned in respect of a tithing which took place in 1283.

An entry in the Gazetteer of Cornwall in 1884 states that it is, *"An ecclesiastical parish formed in 1846 from the parish of St. Agnes, Kea, Kenwyn, and a portion of the ecclesiastical parish of Chacewater.* It is described as, "*A village containing a Wesleyan Chapel, an Inn and about 20 houses.*" It still has the Inn and the village has grown only a little but the chapel has now been converted into dwellings. It has a hotel and a Post Office but in the intervening time, various shops have come and gone and it is now left with no shopping facilities.

It is part of the local government District of Carrick and spans the border of the civil parishes of St. Agnes and Perranzabuloe. The division of the parishes is thought to be more or less in line with Celtic times, before they were joined under Norman rule. This division is marked by Mithian River, which has occasionally been known to flood the lower part of the village. The largest and most populated part of the village lies to the west of the river and up until the early 1900s Mithian Manor owned all of it. This is markedly different from today when the freeholds are mostly owned by individuals. To the east of the river the Vyvyans were the landowners and this included the beautiful Rose-in-Vale.

Mithian has an excellent community spirit and endears itself to all who visit it or make it their home.

The Village Tour

With the passing of years it can be difficult to locate specific houses especially if the names have been changed. To overcome this potential problem, I propose to take you on an imaginary tour when we will come across the houses in a logical sequence. You may, of course, wish to walk the talk and that is not a problem. I have used current place names with the previous, where known, in parenthesis.

There has to be a boundary to the area covered by this book and I have decided that it should be from the present Post Office, on the junction with the St. Agnes and Perranporth road, to the four railway bridges or what is left of them. I know that this will cause some disappointment amongst some of those who live outside of this unilaterally imposed boundary but I had to stop somewhere and maybe there will have to be a second volume.

Mithian is a short distance from the St. Agnes to Perranporth road and that is where we are going to start our journey. Approaching from Perranporth we pass Mithian School on our right and about a third of the way down the steep hill there is a left turn signposted for Mithian. Travelling from St. Agnes we ascend the hill from Barkla Shop, around a sharp left hand bend and a little further up the hill the Mithian turning is on our right.

On the left side of the hill and almost opposite the road into Mithian is **GLEN-CARNE NURSERY,** run by Mr. and Mrs. Crozier. This is located on the site of the former Mithian Women's Institute. The house opposite is also called **GLEN-CARNE** and was built on the site of the carpentry workshop belonging to John Tredinnick of Beacon View.
Immediately opposite the nursery is **MITHIAN POST OFFICE** or **CORNER HOUSE** (Beacon View**).** It was once the home of John and Gertrude Tredinnick and their family. John Tredinnick was born in 1867 and died in 1950 and was certainly a Jack-of-all-trades. He was a carpenter, builder, undertaker, preacher, auctioneer and agent for a shipping company so he couldn't have had much spare time. He operated as a builder during the early 1900s and undertook a lot of work in the area before moving to live in Truro in 1940. Wallace and Edna Evans moved here in 1963 with their daughter, Janet. Mrs. Evans describes herself as a Fen girl, having moved down from Cambridgeshire. As we now turn towards the village we are in Mithian Lane and immediately on our right is some holiday accommodation and a fairly modern bungalow called **THE GRANGE**. This was once the home of Jack and Ronna Chapman and their family following their move from Glen-carne. Prior to the building of the

bungalow it was the base for Jack Chapman's cattle lorry business and the picture shows him with one of his lorries. My thanks go to photographer Ken Young for allowing its inclusion.

It was also the site of Alfred Crebo's (Freda Male's grandfather) blacksmith's shop during the late 1880s to the early 1900s. It is a strange thing to be remembered for but whoever refers to Alfred Crebo seems to recall him having very small feet and wearing size four shoes.

Continuing along the, "Lane" there are fields on both sides and as we approach a slow "S" bend the road gets even narrower. You may notice an entrance to an old lane on our left. This leads to the top of Barkla Hill and once provided a traffic free route to the school. What a boon it would be to today's schoolchildren.

On our right is a pair of semi-detached houses set back from the road. This is **MITHIAN FARM** and many of the buildings near-by were once a part of its holding. During the 1890s it was occupied by Mr. Dale Martin and by 1906, his sisters, the Misses Mary and Annie Martin had taken over from him.

Like most of Mithian, the farm was once a part of the Manor of Mithian and was owned by the Davey family until 1900 when it was sold to John Charles Williams of Caerhays Castle. As part of their tenanted farms policy, Cornwall County Council bought it in 1910 and leased it to a number of local tenants. The main farmhouse was divided into two dwellings each with about 50 acres of land. Mithian Farm Cottage was the third main element with a number of smaller holdings consisting of a few fields.

The right hand side of Mithian Farm house, with its related land, was farmed by Captain Joseph James (Jeff) Hooper in 1923 before he moved to Australia. Stanley Williams then took over and was there until 1938 when James (Jimmy) and Millicent Rowe (née Chapman) moved there and farmed it until 1966. Their elder daughter, Heather was then five or six and her sister, Susanne, was born there.

Courtney Jenkin has lived in the left side of Mithian Farm house since 1932 and there is more about him throughout the book.

To the south west of Mithian Farm is a group of long thin fields, which are probably the remnants of a medieval strip field system.

Set in an enclosed garden is an attractive house called the **MOWHAY**. This is the newest house in the village and its design fits in well with the surrounding buildings. Just beyond is a complex of buildings that were once part of the farm and which have now been converted into dwellings.

In 1976 Cornwall County Council sold most of the farm retaining only the part where Courtney Jenkin lives and approximately forty acres on the left of Mithian Lane. The decision to sell the farm was slightly unusual but was

influenced by the fact that it was so close to the centre of the village. The farm was divided into a number of lots and auctioned. The Wills family purchased the farm buildings and some land and moved into the partly refurbished cows' house. In 1985 they moved abroad and the property was sold at an auction on 4th January 1986 at the Rose-in-Vale.
Barry and Julia Ostler purchased the old barn or corn store and this has now been extended and converted into **THE ROUND HOUSE**. Attached to the main part of the dwelling is the old Round House that is used for Barry's building design practice, Architectural Design Workshop. This section could originally have had some religious use or, more likely, was a whim house where the corn was ground. This would be carried out using two large stones, the top one, being pulled around by a pony or donkey. Cornwall Archaeological Unit confirm that the size of the building compares with a horse whim driven grinding house of the 18th/19th century. The sketch on the previous page shows the Round House before renovation and was drawn by Sonia Fynn for the front page of our village magazine.

The old cows' house was bought by Jen and Alan Roberson and converted into **SOUTH BARN.** Since then, Jen and Alan have separated and she is now married to Paul Nicholls. The farm buildings are well built, using stone from Jericho valley, which may suggest that their original purpose may not have been that of agriculture or that it was a somewhat upmarket animal house. The building has brick arches over the windows, but these may not be original, which give weight to the story that it may have been used, at some time, for a much grander purpose. This could have been as stables to Mithian Manor which is only a short distance away. It could even have been the old chapel, which you will read about later, or a monastery that is often referred to. It is suggested that the field behind this building is an ancient burial ground linked to a monastery but I include that as something that is spoken of and not as verifiable fact.

Following the road to the right reveals the village centre and the early 1900s photograph on the front cover provides a view that has delighted artists and photographers over the years.

On the right and served by a short drive is **WHITEWALLS BARN**, a converted farm building at the end of a short access lane. This was formerly a cowshed but may previously have been a dwelling as an old fireplace was discovered here.

Directly opposite is **PIGGY LANE** (Trewartha Lane or Warra Lane). This connects with the main road on the Perranporth side of the school. A little way up this lane is **TREWARTHA FARM** (Warra Farm).

CCC Monuments Record states that, "*It was first recorded in 1550 and the name is Cornish from, "tre" and "guartha" meaning upper farmstead. It was a tenement of the Manor of Mithian and a full description of the land appeared in a lease of 1728. The kitchens and other rooms of the house were described, together with the garden and a number of fields, including park an min (field on the edge?). Stoney croft, blowing house downs and furzey croft.*"

In 1702 it was occupied by Hugh Tonkin Esq. who is described as a Free Tenant of Andrewartha or Trewartha. There was a famous legal case between him and his landlord, William Mohun, which he lost.

Mr. and Mrs. Roskilly owned it and possibly lived here at some time. Mrs. Roskilly was a Barkla whose father, or other relation, was probably the blacksmith during the 1700s after whom Barkla Shop was named. Martha Barkla, at one time, had a shop, forge and blacksmith shop.

In 1842 there was mention of the Manor of Trewartha. It was approximately 100 acres and farmed by James Ennor who also had the Grist Mill in the valley opposite Rose-in-Vale.

It was rented to Sam Woolcock around 1910 and then to his son, James Woolcock up the early 1930s. In 1933 it was sold to John Mitchell

who farmed it with his son, William (Bill). John's wife, Annie, was a sister to John Berryman of St. Agnes who was well known as a County Councillor and prominent Methodist. The 105-acre holding was a mixed farm and in later years the Mitchells also undertook some contracting. In 1938 machine milking was introduced but prior to this all the milking was by hand. Prior to 1947 an engine and generator powered the milking machine but this was replaced by mains electricity. The Mitchells operated a milk round in the

Perranporth area with two delivery vans and used the slogan, "Mitchell's Matchless Milk" which can be seen on the bottles in the picture. To supplement the supply from their thirty cows they bought milk from other farmers including Mr. Glasson and Mr. Caunter from the village and Stanley Williams who had moved from Mithian Farm to Mingoose Farm. Life was very busy and Bill recalls that the working day started at 5.30am and finished at 9.00 pm for seven days a week. He drove one of the milk vans with the other being driven by George Dyer (son of Tom and Maggie Dyer) but after Bill was seriously injured in a motorcycle accident in 1950 it was not possible to continue and the round was sold.

During the late 1930s John had the bad luck to have a hayrick fire nearly every year. Heather Harvey recalls that all of the villagers would gather to watch the fire and some of the younger children grew up thinking that this was a village event put on especially for them.

John died in 1970 and Bill continued to farm it until he retired in 1979. Ray and Maureen Woodhouse moved here during the eighties when Maureen was the Head Mistress of Mithian School. They sold to the present occupiers, Scott and Emma Kemp, in 1996, from where they operate their Civil Engineering Surveying Company.

The farm buildings in the yard were converted to a dwelling in the early 1990s and the property is now named **TREWARTHA COTTAGE**.

Retracing our footsteps towards the village we turn left, and once again we are facing the village centre. Immediately on our left is **MITHIAN COTTAGE** (The Stores and Mithian Stores) which was built around 1802. The property was extended in about 1982 when a number of rooms were added including the studio where Sonia Fynn did her painting. It was a grocer's shop for many years but in 1991 it reverted back to a dwelling whilst in the ownership of Dr. and Mrs. Hope. It is now the home of Trevor and Rebecca Hough and their young son, James, who purchased it in 1997. You will find more about this property under the section entitled Shops and Businesses.

SUNNY VILLA is next on the left and its design, incorporating full height bay windows, would seem more appropriate in an urban location. It was rebuilt in 1914 by James George Brewer to replace a cottage destroyed by fire.

I am told that Jim Martin was living here at the time of the fire and that the family (Jim, Gertrude and children Ruby, Doris and Florrie) got out with only the clothes they stood up in.

Miss Lottie Luke lived here during the 1930s with her daughter, "Girlie" and her two sons, Ivan (who worked on the buses), and Sylvanis.

During the late 1930s Fred and Beryl Newell began their married life here. Fred died in 1975 and Beryl stayed for a further 12 years. It is now the home of Lorna and Duncan Smith and family.

Since 1988, **LEONORA COTTAGE** (Ivy Cottage) has been the home of Mr. and Mrs. Chitty although their daughter, Jo, had lived here since 1986.

For many years previously it had been the home of the Kellow family. Thomas James Kellow and Sarah Elizabeth Wills were married in 1896 and had five children; Leo Thomas, Horace Ivan who ran the bus service in St. Agnes, Madeline who married into the Penna family, Verona Wills who married Stanley Ennor and Bernice who was the youngest and is shown in the photograph. Bernice lived here all of her life and remained unmarried.

There is said to be a well directly under the kitchen floor which must have been very convenient in cold weather.

Like many Mithian people, Thomas James Kellow had a reputation as a good gardener, probably helped by the Mithian sewage disposal system of bucket and chuck it.

Opposite Mithian Cottage is a row of three white cottages called, appropriately, **WHITE WALLS**. The top two are numbers 2 and 3 Whitewalls Cottages and the lower one is **THE OLD POST OFFICE.** This was the home of Mrs. and Miss O'Leary from the early 1900s. At one time they occupied the lower two and let the very small top cottage.

Mr. Baker lived in the top cottage during the 1940s. He was the "kit-man" for Mithian football team. Mrs. Benney cooked him a pasty every Saturday and in return he cut out the cartoons from his newspaper for her children. Heather Harvey recalls that he was a lovely man. He would buy two ounces of sweets, which were on ration at the time, and give them to her when she passed by. Mind you, she sometimes had to pass by two or three times!

Charlie Mora lived with the O'Leary family from 1909 when aged 6 weeks and in 1934, aged 24, he moved "up country" to work. He is now

92 years old but remembers many of his contempories and much of his time in Mithian. After an indentured apprenticeship at HTP's in Truro he spent his career in the aircraft industry and in 1938 he was in charge of the team that inspected Spitfire production. He is still a point of reference for authors writing about that famous plane.

Jack James lodged with Miss O'Leary for many years and worked at Lambriggan mine. When Mithian Farm was split into tenancies Jack James rented some fields and turned his hand to agriculture.

He had an open top sports car that was the envy of many and this is included on a number of Mithian photographs. It was stored in the old corrugated iron garage below the institute for many years and eventually sold. I am told that Miss O'Leary referred to him as James when she was in a good mood and lodger when she was not.

Jack Rand took occupation after Miss O'Leary and was followed by Mr. and Mrs. Proctor before they moved to Ivydene in 1956.

Ken Young's 1960s photograph of Whitewalls shows the post box outside the centre cottage and the front door of the top cottage blocked up. The boy in the picture is Robert, a son of Desmond Chapman who was the landlord of the Miners Arms at this time.

THE VILLAGE HALL (previously the Men's Institute) was built in 1893 with the help of a donation from John Passmore Edwards of Blackwater. It originally served as a reading room or literary institute for the men of the village. The library was run Mr. Clemens who lived in the cottage attached to the Miners Arms (now a part of the pub).

The usage rules were gradually relaxed to reflect the wishes of the men-folk providing relaxation for the men of the village and respite from the women-folk who were not allowed access. Open every day except Sundays, it provided facilities including a snooker table (purchased from Mount Hawke Institute), darts, whist and, of course, euchre which is a popular Cornish card game. Looking inside the small hall it is difficult to imagine that it was possible to play snooker although the table was only three quarter size.

Ken Symmons recalls playing darts in the Institute and the occasion when someone threw a dart that stuck in Ken Benney's head. Ken Benney was very relaxed about it but his brother, Arthur, took issue with the offender.

The garden at the back and end of the Institute was called, "The Green" and was lost to public use due to apathy when a claim of ownership was made and not challenged; but that was a long time ago.

During the 1970s the hall was rarely used and, in 1985, an application was submitted by the Men's Institute, that the hall be transferred to the Charity Commission for the benefit of the whole village. This was successful and Mithian Village Hall Management Committee was formed with representatives from the Men's Institute (2), the Women's Institute (2), the Cricket Club (1), the Friday club (1) plus 3 others to be appointed at the AGM and they administer the hall on behalf of the Charity Commission.

The snooker table was temporarily stored in the Sunday school and eventually sold for £250 when that building went to auction in the 1980s.

During the 1920s the lower end gable wall of the Institute collapsed and George Dyer rebuilt it with material paid for by donations from the villagers.

The front porch was not part of the original building and by examination of Clive Benney's many photographs we can determine the date of the addition as between 1907 and 1915. Below the hall and bordering the road is an excellent example of Cornish hedging to the raised garden. A village standpipe was once located here and prior to the installation of mains water, the villagers would visit it to draw off water.

The bitmac parking space provides the entrance to a delightful cottage appropriately named **TUCKAWAY THATCH.** This was once a tied cottage belonging to Mithian Farm and is now the home of Derek and Mary Anstis.

Derek is a grandson of Reuben and Lydia James of Lane Cottage of whom you will read more later. The photo shows Derek's Great-Grandmother who lived here in the late 1800s and when Derek bought the property, in the early 1980s, he had no idea that she had previously occupied it.

Maggie & Tom Dyer lived here during the 1930s to 1950s with their children, George, Ken, Pauline and Tom. During World War II Maggie operated an unofficial eating-place nicknamed, by the servicemen from the aerodrome, "The White Elephant Café."

To the rear of Tuckaway Thatch is **MITHIAN FARM COTTAGE.** This was also a part of Mithian Farm and was split off and leased with about 45 acres in 1910 to "Partner" Tamblyn. It was later farmed by Mr. and Mrs. Charles Brokenshire.

The Caunter family took over and farmed it from about 1938 to 1957. Mr. Caunter senior was a local preacher and lived here with his son, Arthur, and family.

Maurice and Avril Chapman moved from Barkla Shop in 1957 with their two sons, Roger and Ian and farmed it for almost twenty years.

The cottage was then left vacant for about a year until Mr. and Mrs. Ward bought it when Cornwall County Council sold Mithian Farm in 1976. They remained here for three years when it was sold to Chris and Maureen Bones who lived here with their children Mandy and Iain until their move to Trenoweth in 1981 where their daughter, Susanna, was born. Barbara and Bob Gilman and their daughter, Katie moved here in 1982 and stayed until 1991 when Kenneth Lee and Anne Brooke moved in.

This sketch of Mithian Farm Cottage was drawn by Sonia Fynn for publication in the village magazine, "Mithian News and Views."

THE OLDE FORGE/TREVENE (Ivydene) was part of Mithian Manor owned by the Davey family and some areas of the building are thought to date from the 16th century. In 1881 it was leased by Richard Davey of Bochym and Elizabeth Maria Williams (sister of William Horton Davey) to Mr. William Henry Tremewan (aged 50), Martha Tyzzer Tonkin (aged 27), his stepdaughter and William Henry Tremewan (aged 21), his son at a rent of £1.10.0 per year. The lease was for 99 years and was arranged after the surrender of a previous lease dated 1834 and the payment of £35.0.0. It includes the cottage and premises at Mithian Town and a field in Mithian Downs.

There was once a large outbuilding on the site of the present garage. It is thought that the main building dates from 1834 or earlier but the rear sections predate this considerably.

It was sold with the remainder of the estate to John Charles Williams of Caerhays Castle in 1900.

During the early 1900s Frederick Evans, a miner, his wife, Julia and their widowed daughter Edith Mabel Ennor, occupied the property. In

Jan 1931 the Williams estate sold it to Mrs. Edith Mabel Ennor and her son, Nicholas Lanyon Ennor. The photograph was taken during the period that Mrs. Ennor ran a shop and her signboard can be seen over the left door.

Nick Ennor operated his carpentry business from here and it is also thought that it may have been the site of a blacksmith's shop at some time.

Following the death of Mrs. Ennor in the mid 1930s and the decision by her son, Nick Ennor, to move away, the lower wing of the house became the home of Will and Annie Tippett. Animal sheds were located at the rear of the house where Mr. Tippett kept his livestock. Annie Tippett died whilst they were living here and Will moved out sometime in the 1930s.

It was the home of George and Laura Bricknell in 1944 and into the 1950s but it was still owned by Nick Ennor until Frederick George Docking (boot maker) and his wife, Doris Melinda, who lived at the Miners Arms, purchased it in 1944 with Mr. and Mrs. Bricknell as sitting tenants. Mrs. Docking was a daughter of Jim Martin who was the landlord at the Miners Arms.

In November 1951 it was sold with vacant possession to Mr. and Mrs. Maurice Stafford Horne and their son, Graham, and they occupied it as, "a single unit with a single garage."

In 1956 they sold it to Gordon and Ivy Elizabeth Proctor who moved down the hill from Whitewalls. It was whilst they lived here that the property became a guesthouse and the name was changed from Ivydene to Trevene. The name change is said to have been prompted by the purchase of linen inscribed Trevene and it was considered easier to change the name of the house than alter the linen. Whilst in the ownership of the Proctors it became the location of Mithian Post Office for a few years.

In 1962 Mrs. Ena Alice Swain, who later married and became Mrs. Holmstrom, purchased it. Considerable alterations and repairs were carried out whilst they were here including a new roof and the removal of one of the staircases.

Mr. and Mrs. William Ernest Mark Drummer purchased it in 1971 and it was they who changed the name to The Olde Forge. They sold it to Red-Oak Restaurants Ltd three years later and Mr. and Mrs. Harry Hill then ran the guesthouse.

In 1979 it was sold to Mr. and Mrs. Chris Targett who ran it as a guesthouse and tearoom until October 1986. The property was then divided into two units with the front part being named Trevene and used as a holiday let until 1989. The rear section was retained for their own use and they continued to call it The Olde Forge. Trevene was sold to Peter Bennett Andrew and Associates in 1990 (Mr. Andrew was the landlord of the Miners Arms) and is now the home of Monika Hunt and family.

On our right is **THE ORCHARD** which was built in 1979 and is where I live with my wife Suzanne (Sue) and daughter Louisa; Andrew, our son, having flown the nest some time ago. The site on which the house stands was an orchard belonging to Mithian Farm.

Turning left and looking down the hill, the post box, telephone, village notice board and seat is on our right. Up to the 1930s, the seat was located immediately in front of The Orchard and was a convenient resting place where the old men would sit smoking their pipes and "putting the world to rights." A number of people have told me that someone, at some time was hanged, drawn and quartered on the village green but I have not been able to find any reference to this or to meet any eyewitnesses.

Just beyond this, is a complex of houses that comprised **MITHIAN MANOR;** considered to be the oldest building in Mithian and certainly, the most historically important. Considering this, I have included a specific chapter to its history and only include here items that relate to more recent times.

There is reference to it being divided into five dwellings; **MANOR COTTAGE** (Brick House) and **FLORAL COTTAGE**, which front the main road, and **THE OLD MANOR** (2 & 3 Rose Cottages) and **POTTER'S COTTAGE** (1 Rose Cottage) at the rear. The three cottages at the rear, formerly Nos. 1, 2 and 3 Rose Cottages, are all now occupied by Jane and Brian Guttridge.

Miss Katie Biddick lived in Potter's Cottage for most of her life, leaving in the 1980s. At that time it was still referred to as 1 Rose Cottage. For those of you who are hoping for a connection with a medieval potter, I have to disappoint you, as the potter after which it was named was Stuart White who lived and worked here for a short time during the mid 1980s.

Miss Day lived in 2 Rose Cottage during the 1930s and in the 1950s it became the home of Mr. and Mrs. Edwin Brokenshire and their family (Mr. Brokenshire was generally referred to as Father Brokenshire). This very small cottage, the home of some large families, has now been incorporated into The Old Manor.

William Badden (a grandfather of Austin Tremain of St. Agnes) lived in The Old Manor during the 1920s/1930s and was a familiar sight as he drove his traction engine and threshing machine to and from the local farms.

Melville Strike and his parents lived here during the early 1950s following which it became the home of Sid Watkins and family during the 1960s.

Nick and Alice Berringer (Alice was the daughter of Mr. and Mrs. Godfrey) purchased the three rear cottages from Ian Chapman in 1978 at which time, Miss Biddick lived in No. 1 and nos. 2 and 3 were unoccupied and in need of renovation. Ian had had the property for about five years prior to which the Bown family of Perranporth had owned it for many years. The photographs show the front and rear elevations just prior to renovations being carried out when a number of old features were uncovered. The room with the circular headed window on the rear elevation was large and had a built up external door that must have had an external staircase to reach it. A short staircase led from what was no. 3 Rose Cottage to Manor Cottage in the front. The floor of the large first floor room was lower at some time and the ceiling had once had large coving (this is very similar to an upstairs room in the Miners Arms). Nick and Alice Beringer sold to Dr. and Mrs. T. M. Geake and moved to Baldhu in 1984.

Floral Cottage and Manor Cottage are probably not as old as the rest of the building but the rear section on its own is unlikely to have been large enough to be a manor. The answer is not clear but it may be that the newer front section was built on the site of a previous building.

Sometime around 1900 Floral Cottage was the home of John Solway who was the grandfather of Irven Solway of Trevellas who is one of my sources of information

Ivan G & Phyllis M Luke were living in Floral Cottage in 1949 (Ivan was a son of Lottie Luke) and were followed by Mary and Norman Roberts during the 1950s. Chris and Jennie Williamson lived here in the mid 1970s and 1980s.

Ida Tippett and her son Leonard lived in Manor Cottage during the 1930s and Ida ran a small shop from here. Florrie Brokenshire moved here in 1947 with her family, Maureen, Pat and John when her husband, Freddie was killed in a farming accident. They remained until 1966

On our left is the famous public House, the **MINERS ARMS**. Up to about the 1960s the wing on the left was a separate dwelling house and, as I have said previously, was occupied by Mr. Clemens who was very involved in the Men's Institute. During the 1950s/1960s Mrs. Warren lived here and is remembered for her love of cats. There is considerable history attached to this building and more on this property can be found in the section on Shops and Businesses.

As we start to descend the hill you will probably not be aware that we are passing over an underground tunnel that once connected the Miners Arms and what is now, The Old Manor. This is historically very intriguing and many people have a view on its possible use. I discuss it later in the book and you may be able to form your own opinion as to why it was built.

This rather steep hill was once known as, "The Lane" and the photograph shows why. Perhaps because of the confusion with Mithian Lane, the name has now dropped out of use. Prior to this it was referred to as Brewery Hill, so named because the brewery horse and drays could not get up the steep hill necessitating the barrels to be hauled up by ropes and the empty ones rolled back down.

On our left is a pair of semi-detached cottages. The top one is called **UNDERWOOD** and was occupied for many years by a lady who was known to all as Granny Bartle and who died in the 1930s. She had four children; Archie and Sidney and their half brothers, John and Tom. Archie was a father to Clyde Bartle who lived outside the village but attended Mithian School. Clyde, who is now 83, ran a grocery store in St. Agnes for some years. Tom was the slaughter man and butcher who lived at Woodlands.

John (Jack) & Mary Rand lived here after the war. Jack was an RAF youth worker during the early 1950s after which the family moved to Canada and he joined the Mounted Police.

George and Elsie Bricknell then moved here (Laura had died and George had married again) and many people can remember Elsie living here long after her husband had died.

The Lower cottage, **LITTLE WILLOWS** (also called Underwood at some time) is the home of Charmian Law and family who purchased it from Liz and Pete Rowe. It was the home of Mr. & Mrs. John King in the 1920s. Mr. King was a carpenter and his workshop was located just beyond the house. He once built a prefabricated outside lavatory for Gum Tree Cottage and the remains of it are still standing. It was, apparently, so big that he could not get it out of the workshop entrance and he had to dismantle it and rebuild it outside. Following the death of his parents their son, John (Jack) King, continued living there until 1974. He was a local councillor and the photograph shows him when he was Chairman of Truro Rural District Council. (photograph by courtesy of Ken Young). He is the author of a short paper on Mithian from which I have quoted. Mr. and Mrs. Godfrey occupied the property after John King moved to St. Agnes and they stayed until 1984 when they moved to Baldhu.

At the rear of Little Willows is a very old perimeter wall enclosing the garden providing us with yet another Mithian mystery. A walled garden seems much too grand to be serving the cottage and suggests that it may have had a much more important use. I don't know the answer to this but there are a few possibilities that spring to mind and you are welcome to adopt one of mine or to come up with your own. There is talk of the existence of a monastery or maybe a monastic retreat in this area and the garden could well have been created to provide produce and to occupy the monks. Maybe, just maybe the Miners Arms once had an altogether different purpose and we can add religious to the other known uses of public house, dwelling, shop and courthouse. Mithian Manor is only the width of a cart track away and the garden may have been built to serve the Lords of the Manor. Whatever the answer, The Manor, The Miners Arms and the connecting tunnel are keeping their secret but undoubtedly they are key to resolving many of the unknowns in this village.

Next down the hill is a pair of modern houses built in 1960. **WILLOW TREE** became the home of Roy and Betty Campbell but, sadly, Betty died whilst abroad on holiday. Betty's parents initially occupied **CLOUDS END** before Mr. and Mrs. Peter Hudson lived there for a short period during 1976/77. Since 1978 it has been the home of Graham and Jennie Dodd and their children, Thomas and Rosalind. The site had previously been an orchard let with Mithian Farm Cottage.

Roy Campbell's son, Andrew, found a Roman coin (D N Gratianus - Gratian AD367-AD383) in the garden of Willow Tree in 1978 and it is intriguing to think that it may have been dropped by a Roman or by a local person who may have been trading with the Romans.

On the opposite side of the road is **KANDO COTTAGE**, a modern house built in the late 1970s by John & Thelma Wilkins and purchased by John and Linda Hewitt in 1985. The plot of land on which it is built was previously a garden belonging to George and Muriel Symmons on which a chalet bungalow had once stood.

THE GROVE (Lane Cottage) is a little further down on the left and was purchased by Simon Hooper (the younger) in 1895. The conveyance states that he was in occupation and had recently erected a cottage there.

There had previously been buildings on this site as shown on the OS map of 1880 and referred to by Jack King in his paper of July 1965 where he states, *"In olden days, in what is now, "Lane Cottage" there were three cottages, one of which was a, "Dame's School." An ancient Cloam Oven can still be found in the corner of the garden."* The oven referred to is still in existence.

In 1897 John Whitford of Rose-in-Vale purchased the lower garden, quarry and woodland bordering the west side of the track now shown as a public right of way to Perranporth and in 1907 he sold it to Simon Hooper. Simon Hooper died in 1911 at City Deep Mine in Johannesburg and left the property to his wife, Julia Jane Hooper who sold it in 1919 to James Dibbs (boot factors mngr) of St. Agnes for £310 and he seems to have changed the name to The Grove. In 1927 James Dibbs, who was by now a grocer, sold it to Harriet Elizabeth Nail of Essex for £445. By 1937, the value of the property had dropped slightly when it was sold for £435 at auction but the price was considered cheap because there were, "very few bidders." It was at this time that the family of the current owners, Phil and Annie Knight come into the picture as it was Annie's great Aunt, Florence Maria Evans, who successfully bid for it. In 1974 Mrs. Evans' nephew, John Flanagan became the owner and he may be familiar to some as he lived there with his Aunt during 1948 to 1952 and attended Mithian School

Around the turn of the century (1900) Reuben James and Lydia James née Hooper lived there. Reuben was from Callestick and went on to become a very successful mining captain in South Africa but died at the early age of 41 in 1914. Soon after their marriage they moved abroad and their first child was born. With the onset of the Boer War the family returned to Mithian but Reuben returned to South Africa after hostilities had ceased. Lydia eventually joined him where their youngest child, Gladys May (mother of Derek Anstis), was born. The 1904 picture shows the house prior to the addition of the veranda and the two children are Pearl and Della who were sisters to Gladys. Lydia was a daughter of Simon Hooper of Mithian and sister to Ann Searle Whitford who lived at Rose-in-Vale.

A more recent view of The Grove from the pen of John Flanagan.

It is probable that we are now accompanied in our journey by the sound of running water. It appears through a hole in the wall that once had a metal flap to stop vermin running back up the pipe. The open gulley takes it down to the river and it once provided a supply of clear drinking water for the nearby cottages. It was built by John Solway and referred to by some as the "Wishing Well."

At the bottom of the hill there are three cottages on the right called, appropriately, **RIVER COTTAGES** (Rose-in-Vale or Vale Cottages).

During World War II the inner cottage was the home of Mr. & Mrs. Gaide and their daughter. From 1955 to 1960 it became the temporary home of Roy and Betty Campbell after which they moved up the hill to Willow Tree. Peter and Brenda Newell then lived here for a few years before Mr. and Mrs. Matthews and their son Tommy who now lives here with his wife, Merla.

Mr. & Mrs. William Brown (Browny) and their daughters Beryl, Hazel and Mavis lived in the centre cottage from about 1910 and Hazel was the last member of the family to move out when she left the village in 1987. Beryl, who is mentioned elsewhere, would have been about 6 or 7 yrs old when they moved in. It then became the home of Vicki and Josh Keep and their family who lived here until the early 1990s.

The cottage nearest the road, **1 RIVERSIDE COTTAGE,** was the home of Fred White and family for some years. He was related to Bill Brown and worked with him on the construction of the railway. He lived here until his death in 1953 when John and Cassie Strike and their son, Melville, moved from The Old Manor. They stayed until the 1980s when Mrs. Strike and Melville moved to St. Agnes.

Roger and Stephanie Chapman (son of Maurice Chapman) and their family have lived here since 1988.

Opposite these cottages is a track that disappears into the woods and after a short distance we find the ruins of **MAGOR'S MILL** (believed to be named after a relation of the Ennor family) and two cottages complete with trees and bushes growing out of the derelict cob walls. Get the timing right and we will see a beautiful carpet of daffodils or bluebells covering the wooded bank that was once referred to as the daffodil gardens. This wooded valley provides an impressive view of The Rose-in-Vale Hotel, a fine Georgian house just across the stream or leat. The gristmill, still in use in the early 1900s, is where local farmers would bring their corn for grinding into animal feed. I imagine that the access road was in a better condition when it was operating – or perhaps not. The Mill was driven by a water wheel, powered by the leat diverted from the river.

The Brown family lived here for a while before moving to River Cottages.

As we return to the road and clean off our shoes, the area on the left is where an old seat and standpipe once stood. This provided a sheltered resting place for the old timers of the village to talk over local issues. Just beyond we again see **ROSE-IN-VALE** Country House Hotel and Restaurant, a prestigious property that is covered in more detail later in this book.

Crossing the road bridge over the river, we are confronted by **ROSE IN VALE COTTAGE**. In 1933 this was sold to Miss Drew of London for £100. Her brother, Horace Drew (nicknamed Cor Blimey), was a greengrocer in Perranporth and used a horse and cart for his door-to-door deliveries. He also attended the local tea treats and fetes where he would sell his produce. In this, he had a rival in Johnny Letcher from Trevellas, and it seems, there was considerable competition that often got out of hand and on one occasion, fists were raised.

During the 1950s it became the home of Mr. & Mrs. Rice, their son Ken, and daughters Sybil and Keitha. Mrs. Nancy Trew and her children lived here during the 1960s before moving to Goshen and in the 1970s it became the home of Mr. and Mrs. Leonard.

Turning left and we are facing a steep climb up Perran Barn Hill. As we pause for breath we can briefly reflect on the difficulties that must have faced our predecessors in carving the narrow, winding roads out of the rocky hillside.

MONTROSE BARN (Perran Barn and Woodyval) is at the top of hill on the left and, as its name suggests, was once part of the buildings of Montrose Farm. A number of people have suggested that it was a religious meeting place, possibly Wesleyan, but I have found no firm evidence of this. Anthony (Tony) and Sandra (Sandy) Jeanette Bonnar have lived here since 1994 and it is a certainly a delightful spot. Tony says that he is still digging up relics from the past when the Rose family used the buildings as implement sheds. He has found various pieces of farm machinery, coal but not the milk churn where John and Norman Rose are said to have kept their money. Many people who paid for coal by cheque never found the amount taken from their bank account and it is thought that their cheques had been placed in this churn. True or not, it makes a good story and perhaps any of you who still have any old churns should check them. Not that you should still have any, of course, as they were recalled by the Milk Marketing Board many years ago but I won't mention yours if you keep quiet about mine!

Montrose Farm was sold in 1983 to Mr. and Mrs. P Woodward who carried out the initial conversion work to this property. In 1987 it was sold to Michael and Jennifer Lynne Jones who undertook further alterations.

Set back on our right is **ROSE MEADOW,** a fairly new bungalow, the home of Ken and Betty Miners and their daughter, Janice. This was built when they retired and moved the short distance from Goshen Farm. Ken and Betty have been an important source of information to me and are mentioned frequently in the various sections of this book.

As we branch left we see a cottage a short distance up the hill to our right. This is **MONTROSE FARM** (Mont Rose or Monterose) and was once the centre of a fairly large farm owned for many years by the Rose family. They also ran a transport and coal merchant business employing quite a few local people. One of their contracts was the transportation of munitions during the 1st World War from Noble's factory, on the Perranporth aerodrome, to Truro Quay. Ken Miners recalls that they had two wagons made for this contract, one by John Tredinnick at a cost of £55 and one by Frank Piper for £50. It was said that Tredinnick's, although more expensive, was superior. The coal business started as a direct result of this contract due to the need for return loads from Truro quay.

John Eley worked part time for John and Norman Rose and recalls them buying full railway wagons of coal which had to be shovelled out by hand at either St. Agnes or Perranporth stations. On some occasions the wagons were not purpose built and the sides were fixed, requiring the coal to be thrown up over the side and the required six feet from the track. A full day's shovelling was needed to unload the 10 ton load for which he was paid 2/6 (12.5p) per hour in the 1960s. The coal was then weighed into sacks and loaded onto the lorries for delivery. John recalls delivering coal to households and that the hours were long involving a late start and an even later finish. Probably his most memorable finish time was after midnight on Christmas day morning. It was this evening when he crossed paths with Arthur Thomas who was still delivering greengroceries.

John Rose was an excellent ploughman and won many ploughing competitions using his "cock-up" (reversible) plough.

The railway and Halt is just beyond Montrose Farm but little sign of its existence remains although the slight dip in the road and the rough ground in the field on the right is a slight giveaway. There is a lovely story that John delayed the railway contractors a day whilst he scraped off the topsoil from the route of the track across his fields (well topsoil can be dearer than saffron).

Montrose Farm was sold by the Rose family in 1983 to Mr. and Mrs. P Woodward and it was split up and disposed of in a number of parcels. The farmhouse and some of the land was purchased by Mr. and Mrs. Squires and is now the home of Dave and Val Daniels who have lived here since 1997.

Continuing our stroll along the lower road, we immediately pass a track disappearing down through the wooded side of the valley. This leads to

LOVELY VALE and is the home of Wendy and Alan Price and, as the name implies, it is a beautiful location. This lane once served three properties but Lovely Vale and Lovely Rose were converted into a single unit in 1967. Just beyond is the ruins of the third dwelling which was very small and called Gum Tree Cottage. This was once the home of a family of nine and water had to be obtained from the nearby stream. Will and Annie Tippett lived here during the 1920s and 1930s after which Frank Skewes and then Mr. and Mrs. Marshall Brokenshire occupied it through to the early 1940s.

In 1921 Sir Courtney Bourchier Vyvyan sold the properties and it is thought that they became tied cottages belonging to Higher Penwartha Farm.

You will have noticed a number of Ken Young's photographs throughout the book and it was interesting to hear that he lived in Lovely Vale for a year in 1926 when he was eight years old. His family had moved to Cornwall and needed accommodation for a short while whilst they found a house. He travelled by train from Mithian Halt to St. Agnes station each day to attend school. He remembers the Bending family living next door.

The Sincock family owned the properties from 1963 and it was Mr. Sincock who converted the two semi-detached cottages into one dwelling. It was sold to Mr. and Mrs. Bernard Sellix in 1968 and, following the death of her husband, Mrs. Sellix sold it to Mervyn France in 1982. Mr. and Mrs. Donald Hardy Bailey then bought it in 1985 and lived there only a year before selling it to Wendy Whitehead who married Alan Price in 1987.

Climbing back up the long access lane we regain the road. As we glance across the valley we are likely to see a number of horses grazing in the fields and it is a sign of the times that they now greatly outnumber the cattle in Mithian.

MOUNT ROSE (Little Montrose) is just a short distance along the road and has been the home of Leslie and Shirley Lobb since 1988. It was the home of the Solway family for many years, following which, Mr. and Mrs. Ernie Brokenshire (the parents of Freddie Brokenshire) took occupation during the 1930s. It then became the home of Jim and Jean Chellew. Mrs. Chellew regularly travelled by train to Perranporth where she would sell her garden produce and if she was too late to walk to the Halt, she would simply jump over the fence and flag down the train. In 1983 it was sold to Arthur Lloyd who converted the near-derelict cottage and cowshed into a large and attractive cottage. He installed an electricity and water supply for the first time but the well that had previously supplied the water was retained as a feature.

Just beyond is the old railway bridge and the granite and metal parts are still evident. The gate on the left is signposted **PENWARTHA BARTON** and the lane is the bed of the old railway track. The fields beyond are known as Solway's Meadows and the hedges have been undisturbed for generations.

Having reached the old railway bridge we now turn and head back to the Rose–in-Vale where we branch left and proceed up the very narrow incline. As we walk up this road and glance to our right we see the wooded side of the valley sweeping down to the river which is rushing on its way to the sea. Just beyond the trees are the old chapel and some houses that we will come across later.

The first house on the left is **GOSHEN FARM.** Mr. & Mrs. Henry Johns occupied this until 1929 when they moved to Wheal Davy Farm at Wheal Butson. It then became the home of George Henry (Harry) & Frederica Miners and their twin sons Ken & Roy who moved here from Penwartha. Following the death of his father, Ken Miners continued to farm the holding until his retirement in 1990 following which the property was sold by the Trenerry family.

GOSHEN FARM COTTAGE is next door and was once part of Goshen Farm. It has been the home of Maureen & Henry Solomon since 1958. During the 1930s it was the home of the Ford family and Florrie & Freddie Brokenshire, who lived here during the late 1930s to 1945, followed them. Next came Arthur Colwill, Fred Biscombe and Ken and Mona Benney in 1951.

Somewhere on our walk you are likely to hear the drone of a plane towing a glider, listen for the change in engine sound as it releases its load and heads back to the aerodrome leaving the glider to continue its silent journey.

Just around the corner there is a lane on the right which leads to two cottages, **BAL GOSHEN** and **PICKETY WITCH** which were once a single dwelling and smallholding. Mrs. May Tippett (Hedley Robert's sister) and her mother lived there in the 1950s. Alice Beringer remembers Mrs. Tippett placing her washing on the gorse to dry, a common practice at that time and one that must have given the items a wonderful smell.

Mr. and Mrs. Godfrey then purchased it, retaining the land (approximately five acres) and selling the dwellings to Mrs. Nancy Trew sometime during the early 1960s. At one time the property was a public house, probably at the time when Wheal Goshen was active.

Whilst we are here, a glance over the left side of the old railway bridge is worthwhile. If you are able to ignore the selfish actions of the fly-tippers you may be able to imagine a steam train enveloping the bridge in smoke as it begins its reduction in speed in its approach to the Halt. Most of the land on the route of the track has been returned to pasture but this cutting remains. Just beyond the bridge, on our left and some distance away, there is an attractive cottage where John and Margaret Eley live.

We can now choose to use the bridge as the limit of our walk or to continue up the hill, past the farm and turn right into a lane that, by turning right again, will bring us down to Mill Pool. Taking the former option, we now need to find our way back to Rose-in-Vale and up the hill to the "square" where, after the long climb, we may be lucky enough to find the Miners Arms open.

Passing Manor Cottage and Floral Cottage on our left we come to **THE HERMITAGE** (The Den) where John and Birgitta (Beta) Varcoe have lived since 1988. The house is thought to date from the late 1500s and at one time it was two cottages but the date of the conversion is not known.

It suffered extensive fire damage in the 1950s but managed to retain its character and charm when rebuilt.

In 1957 Kate Rose Bassett sold it to Edward Stanley Vials who seems to have died in 1976.
It was then sold to Peter and Angela Royle and it was their son, Keran, who drew the sketch of the house and kindly agreed to it being included. After only a couple of years, they sold it to Ray and Geraldine Valteris (or TreValteris as Ray would amusingly call himself) and in 1980 it was purchased by Dennis and Penny Reid who lived here until 1988.

Just beyond the Hermitage, and on the opposite side of the road, is **THE TERRACE** (Kail Alley). The name Kail Alley survived to the 1950s and came from the use of the covered way between two of the cottages as a skittle alley.

According to Jack King's paper, there were two rows of back-to-back cottages here in the 1920s but one by one the pairs have been converted into larger units and there are now only three cottages.

The lower end of the row is now the home of John and Sandra Gillett who moved here in the late 1970s. From 1929 it was occupied by the Benney family. Initially they lived in the rear section of the house but after a few years they also took over the front that had previously been the home of Mrs. Reynolds. At some time during the 1930s a part of this cottage was burnt down and was never rebuilt and there is still signs of where it once stood. During their time of occupation Ken Benney purchased the cottage from Stanley Ennor (Sugs) and it continued to be occupied by their step-mother, Jane Benney, until 1977. Stanley and his mother had occupied the house prior to 1929.

Mr. & Mrs. Harold Lavin and their son Roy once occupied the middle cottage. The Green family moved here during the late 1940s and stayed until sometime in the 1970s. Whilst installing a cesspit or septic tank it was discovered that the ground was so rocky that it was necessary to blast and great care had to be taken to contain the broken rock with wire nets. The extent of the rock is, perhaps, not surprising when you consider the sides of Chapel Hill.

The top cottage (Bakery Cottage) was the home of Mr. & Mrs. Brewer who were the parents of James George Brewer, the haulier from Perranporth. It is referred to as Bakery Cottage because of its use as such in the 1930s and the slate paving discovered in one of the rooms could well have been the bakery floor.

Florrie and Freddie Brokenshire lived here in the mid 1940s but had to move out when Freddie was killed in a farming accident in 1947.

Dick and Edith Harris lived here with their two sons, John and David, from 1953 to 1961 during which time Dick worked for John Rose.

Another hill to climb that takes us from the village to the chapel. In the past it was known as Chapel Hill but, once again, the name is no longer used. The original gradient was much steeper and the rock formation at the sides shows that it has been lowered by a couple of metres. This was probably undertaken in the 1920s. The bottom of the hill was raised in the early 1840s and horses and pedestrians alike must have appreciated the combined effect of the alterations. At one time the sheer sides of the cutting were used to display posters advertising local events.

At the brow of the hill there is a small meadow where James George Brewer's garage and petrol pump for his haulage business was located. Just beyond are the old Chapel and Sunday school which have now been converted into dwellings. This is one of many such conversions in the

locality as a result of dwindling congregations. The photograph is prior to the conversion and, whilst the overall shape has been maintained, it now looks very different. The interior of the old Sunday school, the home of Doris and Christa, has been very tastefully converted.

Immediately ahead is **WOODLANDS,** the location of a former slaughterhouse and butchers run by Thomas (Tom) Henry Bartle from 1914 or, maybe, slightly earlier. He was a son of Granny Bartle who lived at Underwood.

Hedley Roberts was his deliveryman and, after Tom retired, he worked for Tresize Butchers of Goonbell.

James Henry (Harry) Skewes and his wife, Doris, moved here during the mid 1930s and they had one daughter, Gillian (Gill) but unfortunately Doris died shortly after. Harry remarried and he and his wife, Florence (Florrie) had two daughters, Dawn and Irene.

The property was sold in 1978 to George Walsh who carried out an extensive refurbishment before selling it in 1985 to Dr. Bill Smith who lives there now with his wife, Alison. The lane by this property is very narrow and rough but as recently as the1980s it was used for vehicular traffic and was a daily route for the postman's van.

It is quite a pleasant walk down the narrow lane to the foot-bridge over the river which will bring us to a large white cottage called **MILL POOL** where Peter & Nancy Clarke have lived since 1974. Franklyn Ennor lived here at one time but it is not clear whether he was born here or at Magor's Mill.

Mr. and Mrs. Will Tippett moved here circa 1935 and were followed by George and Jessie Hocking, my wife's aunt, who moved out shortly after Jessie's early death in 1946. Following this, George and their two children, Georgina and James, left Mithian and moved to north Cornwall.

Michael Nares Godfrey and his wife, Cecily Edith lived here from 1947 to 1974 and it was the birthplace of their two children, Ralph and Alice (Beringer). Alice recalls it as,, "an idyllic place to spend my childhood." Mr. Godfrey could regularly be seen on the school run carrying a load of children in his Land Rover having negotiated the lane past Woodlands. The vehicle's registration number is NRL 615 and is still owned by his son, Ralph.

In front of the property is the actual mill pool and on our left is the site of a trout farm that operated in the 1970s.

Re-tracing our footsteps and turning left by the old Chapel and Sunday school we rejoin the road. To our left and beyond the small field is an abandoned mine; either Wheal Albion or Wheal Mithian.

A short distance up the hill to our right is **SUNNYSIDE**, the home of Derek Skinner. Derek's parents retired to Sunnyside in 1962 and he joined them during each holiday from his teaching position in Kent. Following his father's death in 1966, his mother lived alone until Derek moved down to join her in 1977. He then spent four years teaching at Truro Cathedral School and a further two years at the Duchy Grammar School before retiring in 1983.

Derek has worked unstintingly for the Village Association of which he has been secretary, treasurer and chairman on a number of occasions. His feeling is that the village became more active from about 1977, which was the date of the Silver Jubilee, when there seemed to be a lot more youngsters about.

This was once the home of William John and Amy Whitford. John's parents lived at Rose-in-Vale and there is more of them later.

At the bottom of the short hill there is a sharp left bend and we will soon see the attractive cottage **MELLOWVEAN** on our left. It was probably built in the 1830s or 1840s and a recently found coin in the structure of the house is dated 1820 and, from its condition, appears to have been lost whilst fairly new.

Geoff and Jenny Osborne have lived here since December 1978 when they purchased it from Clare Otway who, in turn, purchased it from the Misses C. W. & M. B. C. Locke in 1964. They bought it in 1930 and, following renovations, let it to Bert and Lily Skewes who moved here when they were married in 1930. Their daughters Pam (Roberts) and Marlene (Ball) were both born here. Bert worked for Stanley Williams at Mithian Farm until it changed hands at the beginning of the war.

In 1940, Ray and Florence White moved here with their two sons, Ken and Bill. Ray was the Trevellas blacksmith and Ken and Bill both became local musicians. Ken, playing with the St. Agnes and other Brass Bands and Bill, with the Clavatones Dance Band. The Whites moved out in 1964 when Clare Otway made it her home.

The Rice family lived here during the early 1900s and the picture shows the house and family circa 1907. The couple in the doorway are Thomas and Caroline Rice who were born in the 1840s.

On 14th October 1865 a lease was made, "*between Wm. Horton Davey and Richard Davey of the one part and James Ennor .... for the term of 99 years from 25th March 1866 if said James Ennor, Elizabeth Nicholas and Thomas Ennor Courtis should so long live at rent ....*" James Ennor died 9th march 1895 and his wife, Maria, died 27th march 1902. Maria left the leasehold property to her nephew, Wm. Henry May subject to payment of £6 a year.

Almost opposite the property is an old shed in a small enclosure. This is the location of the old cattle pound where stray animals would be temporarily housed and the owner required to pay a fee, or fine, to reclaim the animal.

The next house on the left is **ROSE MERRYN** which is set back some way from the road. Like most of Mithian village, this property belonged to the Manor of Mithian and, in due course, the freehold was sold to an individual buyer. It seems that the Williams of Caerhays sold this property in 1916 to Richard Harris Vincent and his wife Eliza Jane. Part of the dwelling was an animal house at this time. Mr. Vincent died in 1932 and Mr. & Mrs. Charlie Toman lived here until the start of World War II and probably rented it from Mrs. Vincent.

The property was sold to Florence May Richards in 1939 and she lived here for about six or seven years. It then passed to Violet Gumbrell who sold it to Ivan Francis Milton Hine a year later. Mr. Hine sold it again within a few months and in 1947 there begins some periods of longer occupation. Major and Mrs. Adams lived here from 1947 to 1977 when John Teagle purchased it and now lives here with Angelica. John's family own Teagle Machinery Ltd which is based at Tywarnhayle Farm.

There is said to be a ghost sharing the house and Angelica and one of her daughters have both seen it on many occasions. John has not actually witnessed it but has heard unexplained footsteps. Angelica vividly describes it as a young male with blonde curly hair, fine features and blue eyes. He is dressed in working clothes, black trousers and a light coloured or white shirt, which are old fashioned in appearance. He is opaque and when he sits on the bed he depresses the mattress. He is rather timid but has touched her on her shoulder and once placed his hand over her mouth when she tried to ask him a question. She is totally relaxed in his presence and accepts it without fear. Mrs. Adams was also aware of him, and would often say, "My little friend came to visit me last night."

The next field on our left is shown as Parken Crane on the 1840 tithe map (field 1251) and has been described by the CCC Monuments Record, "*By analogy with crane in Gwithian, this can be interpreted as meaning, "field of the fort", derived from "ker bran" "crow fort." However, O J Padel suggests the derivation for Park Crane may be from "Craen " "dam or reservoir." R Warner has suggested it as a possible round site but there are no extant remains. A reservoir here might be associated with the adjacent quarry or mine.*"

Travelling on up the hill we come to an "S" bend where the road travels over the old railway bridge and, again using the bridge as our turning point, we head back towards the village.

The photograph shows a disused water tap located just below Sunneyside. You would be excused for missing this as it is obscured by weeds.

Hopefully, remembering where you parked your car, you leave the village by Chapel Hill, once again passing the chapel as we head out of the village. Negotiating the bridge over the redundant railway, the narrow right hand bend at the top of the incline and avoiding the peacocks at Attwell, you are now in Mithian Downs. After a short distance you will see a road on your right with a sign, "Golf Range" and on your left is a lane leading to Goverley which was the home of Kernick Eley and is now occupied by Ralph and Joan Uglow.
It has been suggested that there was a blacksmith's shop at the entrance of this lane but I have not found any confirmation of this. It is also where the Dymond family lived in their tented accommodation.

Further along we pass **HIGHER MITHIAN FARM** on our right and, after about a half mile a lane on our left, next to Wrinklers Farm, leads to **WHITESTREET.** In Lakes, "Parochial History of Cornwall" we read, "*Of the Roman raised way called Whitestreet, in this parish, little other than the name remains.*" Questions arise of why the Romans would have built a road in this remote area of a county (or country if you prefer) that they did not really occupy.

Community Organisations

Mithian Village Association

There have always been community events in Mithian but since the 1980s most of these have been under the banner of this association. Always seeking to provide an interesting and enjoyable programme of events it has members and officers who work very hard on behalf of the village. Under the heading of events you will see the type of thing that they organise.

There is, of course, an element of fundraising but the prime objective is to make the village an enjoyable place to live.

The chairman and officers of the association are elected at the Annual General Meeting and are ably supported by many villagers who form the committee and undertake the various tasks. The current Chairman is Ken Adams, the secretary is Chris Bones and the treasurer is Derek Skinner.

Women's Institute

Mithian Women's Institute was formed in February 1927 and officially opened by Lady St. Aubyn. Freda Male née Crebo, who was then about seven, presented her with a bouquet of flowers. The members moved into their purpose-built hall on a plot of land given by William John and Bessie Eastlake of Mount May which is the site now occupied by Glen-Carne Nursery. The first annual meeting was held in December 1927 when Mrs. Ichet was elected President.

The full committee were:

Mrs. Bending	Mrs. Brown	Miss M Chapman
Miss Crebo	Mrs. Drew (Treas)	Mrs. Eastlake (VP)
Mrs. Ichet (P)	Miss Ichet (Sec)	Mrs. Jennings
Mrs. Lavin (Asst Sec)	Mrs. Nail	Mrs. Snell
Mrs. Tamblyn (VP)	Mrs. Walker (VP)	

Glancing through the minutes, many familiar names appear as officers or committee members and many interesting events are recorded. The minutes from 1937 show that the programme included items such as dressmaking, gardening, keep fit, precious stones, pottery, literary, sweet making, anti-gas precautions and cake icing. In 1938 the members listened to a talk on the New Government Pension Scheme by Mrs. Fuller.

During the war years the minutes are full of references to the "current difficulties" and of how the W.I. members involved themselves in the war effort. In 1939 a budget, "allowing for heavier expenses due to the war," was passed and the minutes referred to the difficulty in, "planning ahead at present." The 1940 minutes spoke of, "The need for thrift for the use of Home and Country and the need of entertainment – particularly for the airmen stationed within reach." The 1941 minutes record that, "Xmas gifts be sent to all local men in the forces" and that the Red Cross, Rosemundy Home and Truro Infirmary should be supported. An item in the 1945 minutes refers to the use of the hall by Mithian Football Club and this may well be for the joint meeting with St. Agnes Football Club which is mentioned under football. There is also an item regarding the collection of haberdashery to be made for Holland. At the 1949 meeting Mrs. Hussey, President, did the, "good news, bad news" routine. The year had been very successful with thanks going to everyone but the subscription was rising from 2/6 per year to 3/6 per year. Of this, Mithian W. I. retained 1/-, the County 1/6 and the National Federation 1/- (1/- equals 5p). In 1950 someone was beginning to get tough and proposed that, "those who have not paid (their subs) by Jan 31st will be fined the amount of 3d.

The picture shows members with their menfolk from the 1950s and you will probably need a magnifying glass to distinguish the faces.

In 1960 the annual meeting was held at the home of Mrs. Adams, "owing to the state of our hall" and enquiries were to be made about the use of the Men's Institute.

The hall was clearly an asset to both the W.I. and to the village in general with many community events being held there. Freda Male recalls the many concerts, pantomimes and dances that took place there during the war years with the numbers being increased by the airmen from Perranporth aerodrome.

The records show that the structure of the hall was becoming very unsound during the late 1950s and in October 1960 a special meeting was called to discuss its future. Advice and quotations were sought from local builders and many were unwilling to quote or simply stated that the building was in danger of collapse and should be demolished. A decision was made to sell the hall and this took place in 1964 marking a blow to the W.I. and to the village. According to the booklet, "Mithian W.I. 70 years" the sale of the hall raised £159 and this was passed over to the Charity Commissioners.

With no building of their own the W.I. began to temporarily hire the Men's Institute (now the Village Hall) but this must have been very difficult after previously having had their own spacious accommodation. By 1963 the W.I. were ensconced in the Men's Institute but there were concerns at the restricted accommodation and Mrs. Swain offered the use of The Forge for future meetings. Use of the hall has persisted until the present day and must have been made easier with the removal of the snooker table. One thing that has not become easier is the lack of toilet facilities in the hall. Whilst Beryl Newell lived in the village members availed themselves of her facilities but there must have been quite a procession across the road on a cold, winter night.

In 1969 membership had reduced to a handful of people (including Mrs. Godfrey, Mrs. Adams and Mrs. Damsell) and a letter was sent out to all potential members inviting them to attend a meeting. From this point the numbers increased and now stands at about twenty six but has been as many as forty.

In March 1969 Miss Crebo retired from the post of Treasurer which she had held for 36 years.

In 1972 a flowering cherry tree was planted on the village "green" to commemorate Conservation Year but it died recently and has now been removed.

The Queen's Silver Jubilee in 1977 was marked by the planting of red, white and blue flowers outside the Village Hall. Later that year the 50th anniversary of Mithian W.I. was celebrated with a Dinner at the Rose-in-Vale.

In 1985 a new competition was introduced with a shield award in memory of Bernice Kellow.

The club is still very active and organises an annual fete, coach trips and monthly speakers. The current officers (Spring 2003) are President – Betty Miners, Vice President – Pat Ely, Secretary – Val Holderness and Treasurer – Joan Jones.

I am grateful for having been given access to the meeting minutes that have been so meticulously recorded. The minutes of meetings are often the cause of derision or impatience but they are slices of history and make quite fascinating reading. I have also been pleased to include a few recent items from the Mithian W.I. 70-years booklet.

Wesleyan Chapel

Mithian Chapel was built in 1836, about the same time as the chapels at Silverwell and Trevellas. There is reference to Sunday school gatherings in 1815 but I have not been able to find where they met. At a time when religion played a bigger part in people's life and was so relevant to the community the new chapel had a major impact on the village.

In 1911 Captain John Whitford of Rose-in-Vale donated a new organ and John Tredinnick undertook the installation. At the same time new seating was installed and a general refurbishment carried out. As with any project there must have been some tension within the committee responsible as one of the members told one of his colleagues where to put the organ and the other replied that he should go up there and play it!

A report in the Royal Cornwall Gazette on 30th May 1912 stated that, *"A new organ which has been put in the Mithian Wesleyan Church was dedicated on Saturday afternoon by the Revs. W Hodson Smith, supt, of the North Cornwall Mission and G W Thompson. Previous to this service there was a public luncheon, which was largely attended. After the dedication service Mr. Tonkin, organist of Newquay Wesleyan Church, gave an organ recital, and in the evening the Newquay Wesleyan choir gave an excellent musical service. The organ, which was built by Messrs Moon and Sons, of Plymouth, and gave every satisfaction on Saturday, has the following stops .... About £25 was raised during the day."*

Tea Treats are no longer held in Mithian but, like so many Cornish villages, they were once a major event in the annual calendar. A number of locations have been used for the Wesleyan Chapel annual Tea Treat but the field on the village side of Trewartha Farm became known as, "Tea Treat Field." Prior to it moving there it was held in Moor Field, by the Rose-in-Vale. When the move was made up the hill it caused some discontent and, under cover of darkness, Bill Brown and friends moved the stalls and farmers wagons, which were set up for the bandstand, back to the field at Rose-in-Vale. On the morning of the event there was the unexpected task of moving everything back up the hill again to, "Tea Treat Field."

The musical entertainment was always provided by a brass band and the popular recollection is that it was always Camborne Town Band that attended. They were certainly the premier brass band in Cornwall and Franklyn Ennor and his cousin, Stanley, would always insist they were booked as they made, "an ansum sound." Prior to and after their period of influence however, a variety of other bands undertook the engagement as the following extracts from the Royal Cornwall Gazette will testify.

28th May 1903 – *"Mithian Band of Hope on Saturday was a great success. Headed by the Blackwater Band, the members paraded the village, afterwards partaking of tea. Various games were indulged in until 7.00pm when the choir of the Crosscoombe Chapel gave a sacred entertainment in the chapel. A large number attended and greatly appreciated the singing of the choir."*

2nd July 1903 – *"Mithian Wesleyan held their Sunday School Treat on Saturday. The Foxhole band rendered a good selection of music.*

19th May 1904 – *Mithian Band of Hope fete on Saturday was a success. The members paraded the village and afterwards had tea together. Games were indulged in to the cheerful strains of Blackwater Band."* (I recall the Blackwater Band bass drum being stored in the roof of Ward's Garage at Blackwater during the early 1950s which was sometime after the band had broken up).

6th June 1907 – *"Large numbers went to Mithian on Saturday to hear the Camborne Town Band, and to witness the sports, held in connection with the Mithian School tea."*

1st July 1909 – *"St. Agnes Band, under Mr. John Paull, were engaged at Mithian on Saturday, attending the annual tea of the Wesleyans Sunday School."*

30th June 1910 – *"Mithian Wesleyans held their annual Sunday School Tea Treat on Saturday. Treviscoe Band was in attendance."*

30th May 1912 – *"Mithian Band of Hope held their annual demonstration on Saturday, and after parading the village the members enjoyed tea in the open. St. Agnes Band, under Mr. H Robins contributed a musical programme."*

27th June 1912 – *"Heavy rain completely spoilt the Mithian Wesleyans Sunday School tea on Saturday. The children had their tea outdoors and just as the tables were prepared for the teachers, elder scholars, and visitors, down came the rain and spoilt the gathering. St. Agnes Town Band, under Mr. H Robins, was engaged for the afternoon and evening."*

18th June 1919 – Caharrack Band were engaged for the Tea Treat.

The Tea Treats continued for many years and, whilst I can recall playing there with St. Agnes Band in the 1960s, more often than not, they did feature that famous band from Camborne. Ken Miners recalls that in the 1930s, Camborne band charged £11 for the day, quite a lot of money in those days.

The initial part of the Tea Treat consisted of the traditional parade led by the Sunday school banners. This was followed by the band and, what seemed like, the entire village. The route of the parade was from the field, circling Mithian Farm house, to Barkla Shop where the band would play a piece or two. It then made its way back to Rose-in-Vale where the children would be given sweets and an orange before returning to the field. Whilst the band played there would be traditional races, Serpentine Walk, Tea Treat (saffron) bun and tea. Jack Chapman (father of Jack & Maurice) usually served the tea which was made in a large urn. He also supplied the buns.

A number of other locations were later used including the field below the chapel, (White's field) belonging to Geoff and Jennie Osborne and Mrs. Chapman's chalet field. Many may remember White's field also being referred to as Tea Treat Field.

Ken Benney recalls attending Chapel and Sunday school three times on Sundays and of singing, "The Old Rugged Cross" as a solo at the age of four. He also remembers calling to see Mrs. Brewer in Bakery Cottage after the service and having to tell her about the sermon. No chance of him falling asleep!

As I have said previously, the Wesleyan Chapel was a major part of village life as the following reports from the Royal Cornwall Gazette of 23rd May 1907 show:

"Large congregations assembled at Mithian on Sunday to hear the Rev. G W Thompson, who came down from Chatham to conduct the anniversary services in connection with the Sunday school anniversary. Mr. J Angwin presided at the organ. The evening service had to be held in the open, hundreds being unable to gain admittance to the chapel. The secret of Mr. Thompson's power is that he knows the very life of the people."

"School anniversary services were held by Mithian Wesleyan on Whit Sunday. Mr. W J Bennett of Newquay, was the preacher, and a flower service in the afternoon was in the charge of Miss Edith Rogers. Mr. J Berryman presided, and Mr. A Solomon was at the organ."

The RCG also ran a report on the 25th August 1910 saying that,"Mithian Christian Endeavour had a picnic at, "Love's Valley on Saturday." I had no idea where this was but Clive Benney came to the rescue and pinpointed it as a grassy valley about 100 yards from Trevellas Beach when walking towards Cligga Mine along the coast.

From the records of 1935 and 1936, kept by Mrs. Alma Butson née Retallack we can tell that the chapel was very active and well attended. The choir for the evening service of Sunday 21st April 1935 were Mr. Harris,

Mr. Skewes, Mr. Luke, Mr. Kemp, Mr. Ennor, Mrs. Brokenshire, Mrs. Shugg, Mrs. Rice, Mrs. Miners, Mrs. Harris, Mrs. Kemp, Mrs. Piper, Miss Luke and Miss Brokenshire. Mr. Penrose, Mr. Tippett and Mrs. Drew were absent. The organist was paid 7/- of which 1/6 was taken from the Choir Fund and the remainder from contributions by the choir.

In March 1935 there was a concert that included solos, duets, monologues, recitations and a sketch entitled, "Is he married?" Many of the adults of the village took part as did the children and the names of Ken Benney, Arthur Benney, Ken Symmons, Courtney Jenkin, Roy Lavin and many others are shown to have contributed with items.

The programmes for the Anniversary Whit Sundays of 9th June 1935 and 31st May 1936, the Harvest Festival service in 1936 and the Children's Prize Day of 4th January 1936 are recorded but have not been reproduced in this book. Mrs. Butson has also recorded details of the services providing dates, attendance, name of preacher and amount of collection. I have not included this list but the following summary may be of interest. The attendance at morning service averaged about 15 people whereas the evening service was in the region of 50. On a number of occasions there were well over 100 and for the Harvest Festival services of 13th September 1935 there were 54 for the morning service and over 250 for the evening. On that day the collection was £7/8/6 whereas the average per week was about 9/-.

Mrs. Butson also recorded other items of village life in this book including:

14th April 1935 - Leonard Tippett was buried.
13th July 1935 - Willie Gilbert was killed at St. Georges Hill, Perranporth.
14th December 1935 - S Ennor was married.
21st December 1935 – There was a Christmas Tree bazaar.
29th December 1935 – There were severe rain and gales.
15th January 1936 – A concert was given by Crosscoombe friends.
19th February 1936 – Mrs. Bending died.
26th March 1936 – Mrs. Ennor buried.
7th April 1936 – Mrs. F Ennor buried.
19th April 1936 – Summer Time begins.
8th May 1936 – Rhodda White died.
13th June 1936 – Sunday school Tea Treat with Camborne Band (nice weather).
20th June 1936 – Mr. Atkins buried.
27th June 1936 – Mingoose Tea Treat with St. Agnes Band (lovely weather).

18th July 1936 – St. Agnes Tea Treat (Bad Weather).
1st August 1936 – Granny Yelland died.
9th August 1036 – St. Agnes Hospital Sunday with St. Agnes and Queens Bands (lovely weather)
28th September 1936 – Arthur Thomas and Peggy Higgins married at St. Agnes Chapel.
4th October 1936 – Peggy Tredinnick married to Jack Libby at St. Agnes Chapel.
11th October 1936 – Mrs. J Tredinnick buried at Mt. Hawke (Stanley Ennor's Aunt).
4th November 1936 – Mr. Roskrow buried at St. Agnes (knocked down with bicycle at Redruth 31st October).
21st November 1936 – Honor Chapman married to Jim Davey.
26th November 1936 – Emma Tredinnick buried at St. Agnes.
5th December 1936 – Ivy Gilbert knocked down by bicycle at Barkla Shop.
10th December 1936 – King Edward VIII renounced the throne.
12th December 1936 – George VI proclaimed King.
25th December 1936 – I finished playing the organ. Mr. Badcock is the newly appointed organist.

Many concerts with Male Voice choirs filled the place are were usually organised by Franklyn Ennor who would have "nothing but the best." Russell Fowler recalls being MC at a concert by Carnon Vale Male Voice Choir when one of his jokes may have been taken a bit too seriously. He asked a person if they had used a courting machine, to which they enquired what it was. Russell explained that it was a candle in a jam-jar and the other person said that he had not. The response was that it was a pity as he would have seen what he was getting! He was not asked again.

The West Briton on the 18th February 1982 ran the following report regarding a recent service, *"For the first time in many years a family service was held in Mithian Methodist Church on Sunday morning. The speaker was Mr. Brian Dunn, headmaster of Richard Lander School. The lessons were read by Katie Beringer, Mandy Bones and Tom Fynn. A children's choir accompanied the service with solos by Lisa Beringer, Emma and Sarah Targett. The pianist for the choir was Janice Miners and the organist for the service Mrs. Lynn Hewins. The congregation of nearly a 100 included a contingent of Brownies and Guides from St. Agnes."*

The chapel closed in 1983 and many local Methodists transferred to other chapels including "Big chapel" at St. Agnes. The building was sold at auction for £39,000 and converted to dwellings in 1986/7. The beautiful organ sold for only £35 (not £35,000 as quoted in some other books) there being only one bidder present and it is said that he only wanted to use the pipes. The proceeds of the sale were eventually distributed to Methodist Chapels at St. Agnes and Perranporth and to Mithian Church.

St. Peter's Church

The Gazetteer of Cornwall 1884 states that Mithian is, *"An ecclesiastical parish formed in 1846 from the parish of St. Agnes, Kea, Kenwyn, and a portion of the ecclesiastical parish of Chacewater. The Church of St.Peter is situate in the centre of the parish, 4 miles northeast of Redruth, and consists of a chancel, nave, transept, porch, and a handsome tower and spire containing one bell. The living is a vicarage, yearly value £300, in the gift of the Bishop of Truro and Crown respectively; held by the Rev. John McWilliams Bamfield."*

Only four years later, in 1898, the, "handsome tower and spire" were demolished due to crumbling stonework. The tower was rebuilt in 1928 and is used as a trigonometrical station.

In the 1950s I attended Sunday school at St. Peter's and on one occasion my brother and cousin were allowed to climb the stairs to the top to take in the magnificent view but being four years younger, I was considered too young for the climb.

The Rev. Alfred Lord, appointed 9th March 1847, was the first incumbent and was left to make his own arrangement to raise the necessary funds and to build a church and vicarage. The original name of the new parish was Silverwell, but owing to the diminishing importance of that village due to the mine closures the name was changed to Mithian. Having found by measurement the centre of the parish, the Rev. Lord decided to build the church on that spot.

In a letter to the RCG (Royal Cornwall Gazette) on the 4th November 1859, Alfred Lord stated that, *"This district was formed under, "the Peel Act." The population consists with very few exceptions of 2,000 working miners and farm labourers. It was taken out of the parishes of Kenwyn, Kea, St. Agnes and Perranzabuloe."* He goes on to appeal for financial support stating that, *"A most suitable eligible site, two acres, has been kindly given by Messrs. S. and K. Davey."* From money raised so far, a

school-room (licensed for divine worship) and a temporary parsonage had been provided. He requested that subscriptions be sent to him, as the incumbent of Mithian, or to the Cornish Miners Bank or the Devon and Cornwall Bank at Truro.
In Lakes, "Parochial History of Cornwall" it states that the Church was built by voluntary contributions but it is also said that the people of the Parish did not approve of the location and contributed only £20 towards the total cost of £1,322.

Things were obviously moving quite quickly as on the 18th November 1859 an advertisement appeared in the newspaper for, "Persons desirous of contracting for BUILDING a CHURCH for this District ...." From time to time a report of funds raised and from whom they were received, would appear in the RCG.

On the 15th June 1860 the RCG reported that the corner stone of the new church was laid by the Archdeacon of Cornwall and a bottle containing coins of the current reign, and a parchment recording the ceremony, was placed beneath it. The report went on to say, "*During the first 20 years of the 1800s, the building of new churches was rare with proprietary chapels for the rich, meeting houses for the middling classes, leaving the poor to shift as they could. But when God had visited the nation with famine, discontent, and civil strife in 1817, the Government and Parliament became convinced that the alternative was more churches or more prisons; moral control or the bullet and the halter.*"

The walls were already nine feet high in some areas and the stone, thus far, had been from Mr. Hodges quarry near the Four Burrows. The report states that, "*the spot commands a fine and extensive view .... The cultivated valley commencing at Silver Well, and stretching by Rose-in-Vale to Perran Coombe .... The access is most convenient for the old London road from the west to Mitchell and Queens, and the turnpike road from Truro to St. Agnes, intersect each other close to the church.*"

On the 23rd November 1860 a report states that, "*the roof is almost complete and work on the tower is to resume after Christmas.*" The ground for the churchyard was being enclosed and, "*Every effort will be made to have both Church and Churchyard ready for consecration by the latter part of next spring.*"

It seems that even at this late stage in its construction, there was some lingering concern regarding its location as Alfred Lord writes an open letter to the RCG explaining the decision. He considered that he had built it in a position that made it within reach of the whole of the parish which building it in the sheltered hamlet of Mithian or the thickly inhabited village of Blackwater would not. He went on to say that it was his eventual wish to build small Chapels at Mithian and Blackwater.

In January 1861 progress was good and it was said that, "work on the tower would resume with the return of favourable weather."

The consecration of the Church took place in October 1861 and it is clear that the location had been turned from a desolate waste area to a thriving place of beauty. The RCG provided the following account of the Church: *"The Church is crucifix in plan, having chancel and nave, with shallow transepts, south porch and western tower, and spire; a small vestry being appended to the chancel on the north-east. The walls and roofs are lofty, and the interior effect spacious – the nave being * feet wide, and the chancel * feet; their lengths being * feet and * feet respectively."* (it seems that the editor forgot to revisit the report and include the dimensions). It continues, *"The window-sills are kept well up from the floor. The style generally is that of the Early Geometrical Period, the window tracery being simple, and of simple section, whilst the walls are thick, and the splays and inner arches consequently deep and massive. The walls are built of local rubble stone; the dressings of Chacewater elvan, with mullions and sills of St. Stephens granite. The pavements are of slate, with borders of tiles; the flooring of solid wood blocks, or bricks, forming a noiseless and pleasant floor, laid after a manner of pavement. The interior is arranged chorally, and a fitting pulpit and lectern are provided at the East end of the nave. The font is octagonal, of simple design, with a high cover. The roofs internally are of open deal timber work, and externally are covered with small slates. The Eastern gable of the nave is surmounted with a cross of well-wrought iron. The other gables are to be furnished with stone crosses so soon as the available funds for their erection shall be forthcoming. The extreme simplicity of the finish of the building generally calls most strongly for these adjuncts, even in an architectural point of view, and apart from higher consideration; and it is to be hoped that they will not long be wanting. The accommodation of the Church is for *, including * children. The total cost is about £*, towards which amount £* has been contributed by the Ecclesiastical Commissioners, and £* by the Incorporated and Diocesan Church Building Societies. The contract has been efficiently carried out by Mr. W. W. Salmon, of Truro under the architectural supervision of William White, Esq. of London."*

There is no record of a building being used as a place of worship prior to 1861.

In a letter to the RCG on the 20th January 1863, Alfred Lord talks about an anonymous donation towards the cost of building the Parsonage. The schoolrooms are under construction and Mrs. Joseph Boyd, of Probus has been engaged as schoolmistress at a salary of £35 per annum.

An RCG report in February 1863 lists the contributions towards Mithian School and includes the following statement, *"In the last letter addressed to the Public through the medium of this Journal, respecting the works at Mithian, the claims of the Architect for Mithian Parsonage, and other incidental costs were somewhat hastily overlooked. In defence to the judgement of Friends it is now respectfully announced that any contributions for these purposes would be most welcome."* A further report one month later states that, *"The school opened on the 2nd February last with only 10 scholars, now numbers one hundred and one – accommodation for increasing numbers is much required. An Evening School has also been opened at which thirty-six scholars attend, many more will, doubtless, soon enter their names."*

A letter by Alfred Lord in June 1864 to the RCG refers to the state of the tower. He states, "...... *a rather widely-circulated report that the tower of Mithian Church was in danger, owing to the existence of a crack between the belfry door and window, and the splitting of a quoin or two."* He enlisted the help of Mr. Ewan Christian who inspected it and pronounced that it was perfectly safe and that no remedial work should be undertaken. The vibration of a peel of bells would not affect it and all of the movement in the stonework was perfectly natural.

On the 22nd February 1880 the Rev. Alfred Lord, Vicar of Mithian died having achieved much in his lifetime. The RCG reported in September 1882 that, "....... *some interesting and important improvements have been effected in the chancel of the parish church here, the east window having been filled with stained glass of great beauty by the well known artist, Mr. Horwood, of Frome-Selwood, and the walls of the sanctuary richly decorated by the same skilful hand. The whole of the work has been done at the expense of certain members of the family of the late Rev. Alfred Lord (for thirty-three years vicar, and the first Incumbent, of Mithian) and of his second wife; and the parishioners generally, and in particular, the present energetic vicar, the Rev. J. R. Mc Williams Bampfield, may be heartily congratulated on the result."*

In September 1881 a new organ, built by Messrs Hele and Co., of Plymouth, at a cost of £175 was opened. Apparently the money had been, *"cheerfully subscribed and the vicar now contemplates adding an efficient heating apparatus to the church, which is much needed, the situation being very high and bleak."*

On 22nd August 1889 the RCG reported that the roof and windows and spire of the church being in a very unsatisfactory condition, Mr. J. P. St. Aubyn, architect, was asked to inspect the church and report on it. A bazaar was held at Perranporth to raise funds for rebuilding at which the Perranporth band played. The condition of the structure must have been bad as it is reported that, *"Wet streams down the walls of the tower inside and of the south transept and occasionally through the roof on to the seats, and when the wind blows the church is so full of draughts that delicate people avoid it and hardier folk button up their great coats and wish that they might wear their hats."*

The tower and spire were safely demolished in 1898 by Mr. W. Larkins, steeplejack, of Bow, London at a cost of £54. It had been feared that the tower would collapse so its removal must have caused much relief. The bell was temporarily housed in a wooden structure until rebuilding could be undertaken.

In 1921 a grand garden party and fete was held in a field at Tywarnhayle Farm (courtesy of Mr. Teagle). The proceeds were for enlarging the church school. *"St. Agnes band was in attendance and dancing was indulged in."*

In 1924 a beautiful oak rood screen was installed in memory of the late vicar, the Rev. Benjamin Smart.

The replacement tower was built in 1928, using stone from Wheal Daniel, a gift from Lord Falmouth, and granite dressings from St. Austell. The Bishop of Truro dedicated the new tower and formally unlocked the tower door

In 1958 the parishes of Mithian and Mount Hawke became a united Benefice.

There are many instances of walking funerals to the Church when the cortège would slowly make its way from the village and the mourners would take turns to carry the coffin. During the early years the route from Mithian may well have been through Mithian Woods and the lanes that lead to Silverwell.

Whilst on this subject, mention must be made of the double funeral of Joseph Hoare, cattle dealer from Skinner's Bottom, and his housekeeper and lover, Mrs. Laura Sara. They were bludgeoned to death on the 25th January 1920 and, despite the assistance of Scotland Yard, the murderer was never found. The newspaper report states that, *"The cortege proceeded to Mithian Churchyard, about a mile and a half away. Hundreds of people followed on foot, and in addition to a number of carriages, there were over thirty gingles and market traps."* The Rev Benjamin Smart officiated at the service.

The Church still stands alone and, if it had been thought that the communities would extend to encompass the Church, then the collapse of mining activity and the consequent mass migration of the mid and late 1800s put paid to that. The current Vicar is the Rev. Alan Bashforth who also presides over St. Agnes and Mount Hawke parishes. He is working with parishioners to find some ideas to help preserve the Church and a number of open days are being held to progress any ideas.

The Old Mithian Church

This is said to have stood at the western entrance to the village and to have been converted into a farm building. Could this be another reference to Mithian Manor Chapel or could it be another lost church? I have already mentioned that South Barn may have had some religious use and that the Round House could have been a meeting place. We do not know where services were held prior to the building of St. Peter's Church but of course, the new church does not relate just to the village of Mithian.

Whitestreet Wesleyan Chapel

In the early 1900s there was a Wesleyan chapel in use at Whitestreet and its ruins are shown in the picture below.

Mithian Junior and Infants School

Paul Parkinson has been the headmaster for the past seven years and is justifiably proud of the school. He recalls his first panic when, in his initial week, a herd of cows decided to take over the sports field.

The school has 80 to 90 pupils and is divided into three classes taught by Barbara March, Barbara Read and Sioned Young. There have been some recent alterations to the building, which has made it a very light and cheerful place in which to learn. There were no regrets when the old toilet block was, at last, demolished in 2000.

The school participates in many community events including the Furry Dances, Lowenda Perran and various celebrations in the local churches and whilst the three Rs are very important, school activities are broad and cover many items beyond that required by the National Curriculum. The children enjoy taking part in a variety of sports and have achieved some notable success.

The school was built on part of Cold Harbour Farm and was opened on 13th July 1874 with Mr. P Richards as Headmaster and with about fifty children with an age range of five to fourteen. It was designed to receive 200 pupils and was named Buckshead School until about 1930 when the name was changed to Mithian School. Children soon transferred from the Church school (which closed in 1880) and a private school in Mithian and the number quickly grew to well over a hundred.

Education was not free at first and in 1874 it was 1d per week for up to seven year olds and 2d per week for seven and older. By 1880 this had risen to 4d per week for the under fourteens, 6d for fourteen and fifteens and 9d for over fifteens. No payment meant that you were excluded from the class but in 1891 school fees were abolished and education was funded by taxation.

Looking through the admission register I came across many familiar names of Mithian past and I appreciate having the opportunity to examine this.

Truancy was a problem in the early days when children were kept at home to help on the farms with preparing the fields and harvesting. In "Friendly Retreat" by M H Bizley there is reference in 1884 to St. Agnes schoolboys being detained after school for playing truant. It says, *"They went to Mithian to fight the boys there, who had sent them a challenge."* No names were given and it was not recorded which side won!

In 1882 an Inspector's report describes the singing as, "very painful" and I am assured that is not the case now.

The Royal Cornwall Gazette ran a report in the 11th May 1905 edition that suggests that things had improved somewhat. In it, Mr. E Joad, his Majesty's Inspector of Mithian (mixed) Council School says, *"This school is in the main well taught. Written work is neat, and composition is of more than average merit; but more variety of treatment is needed in the arithmetic of the lower standards. Needlework should be taught according to a graded and progressive scheme, which should include practical instruction in cutting out, the girls to fix their own work. The infants' class is on the whole satisfactory in character, though a further knowledge of numbers might be looked for as a result of the year's work."*

During early December 1907 the Royal Cornwall Gazette reports that, *"Mithian Council schools are closed for another fortnight, owing to the prevalence of whooping cough."*

The same newspaper, on 19th January 1911, runs a report of the appointments of new headmasters at Mount Hawke and Mithian. *"St. Agnes managers of the Council Schools met on Thursday, Mr. John Hitchens J.P.*

presiding to appoint headmasters to Mount Hawke and Mithian Schools, vacated by the removal of Mr. J Radcliffe and the lamentable death of Mr. J E Tremewan respectively.

The County Council sent down six names from which to make the selection.. .... After the candidates had been interviewed, a ballot was taken with the result that Mr. Roskrow was appointed to the Mithian School and Mr. Oates to Mount Hawke."

In 1912 a dairy school opened in Mithian but where I do not know.

In 1929 Mithian became a junior and infants school with the older children transferring to other local schools.

1931 saw the closure of the butter making classes.

Ken Miners remembers schooldays in the 1930s when work was still written on slates with chalk. During this period Miss Roskrow, who was the Head Teacher, taught the infants and Miss Fanny Lockett, who later succeeded Miss Roskrow as Head Teacher, taught the juniors. Miss Lockett was a sister to Claude Lockett, who worked for the Water Board, and to Jack Symon's wife (licensee at the St. Agnes Hotel).

On the 11th July 1940 the numbers increased by the addition of war evacuees from Tottenham, London, an occurrence that could have raised many problems but did not. With them came their Headmaster, Mr. F. Moore who lodged in the Miners Arms. David Docking, who attended the school at this time and who lived in the Miners Arms, recalls being quite peeved by this arrangement.

Maureen Solomon recalls the Dymond family attending Mithian School and bringing with them their pet adders, mice and ferrets. The party piece seems to have been when the ferret entered their left jacket sleeve and exited the right. There was always plenty of work to be done outside of school hours and many children took advantage of the arrangement whereby they were allowed a couple of weeks off during the year to help with seasonal farming work. This may have been potato picking, clearing the field of stones, harvesting etc.

Over the years the village Parent Teachers Association (now the Friends of Mithian School) has been very active in raising funds and organising social events. An innovative idea in the 1980s was for the teachers and parents to present concerts for the children. I can confirm that the copious amounts of wine consumed at the rehearsals and performance was for medicinal purposes and was essential to overcome stage fright.

During the 1980s a 24-hour sing-in for school funds was held in the Miners Arms when, "Trelawney" was sung every hour on the hour. Peter Andrew was the landlord at that time and was extremely supportive of the event.

Many of the people mentioned in this book attended Mithian School including four generations of my wife's family. Her Grandfather Edward John Roberts attended in the 1800s, her father, William John (Jack) Roberts started on 16th November 1914, Sue started in 1951 and our children, Andrew and Louisa attended in the 1980s.

Prior to the state school opening there were a number of private schools offering education at a price. One such school was in Mithian Woods, between Millpool and Park Hosken, and the ruins are still visible. Jim Batten is said to have attended there and as he was an old man in 1930 it was probably running during the 1850s.

Football

Sadly, Mithian no longer has a football team but during the early 1940s, Mithian had one of the best teams around and competed well in competitions including the Dunn Cup and the Junior Cup. The highlight seems to have been the defeat of the GPO team from Truro who had not lost a game for three seasons.

Even prior to this period there was football in Mithian and Charlie Mora recalls Tom Dyer being captain. He would often be heard issuing instructions to the team to, "Ignore the ball and play the man!"

Various pitch locations are recalled and during the 1930s it was on the left side of Mithian Lane (heading from the village to the Perranporth/St. Agnes road) but later switched to the other side.

Russell Fowler played in the 1940s team for about three years and some of the names that he recalls are listed below. It does seem to have been a sort of "League of Nations" as many of the players were from outside Mithian. He recalls not being too interested at first and he played his first match using ordinary shoes as he had turned up to watch and been co-opted due to a shortage of players. He couldn't have been too bad as he then became a regular team member. The pitch at this time was on the left after passing Avril Chapman's bungalow. It now belongs to Bernard and Carole Hoskins and is remembered as being called, "Goodseth" or something similar. There were no changing facilities but sacks were provided to cover up the players' clothing in the event of rain. After a while a disused pigsty on the other side of the road was brought into use, after it had been cleaned. Russell is not sure who actually picked the team but Franklyn Ennor, Stanley Ennor and George Bricknell seemed to be in charge. In those days, substitutes were not allowed and during one match, Chick Edwards had a bad head wound early in the game. He was rushed to St. Agnes to see Doctor Whitworth who patched him up and he returned to play the second half. In the event of a leg injury you were put in goal and Russell Fowler, who is somewhat vertically challenged, recalls this happening to him when he failed to make his height count and let in sixteen goals against the dreaded GPO team. He also recalls being dumped behind a goal after breaking his ankle and being forgotten by the rest of the team when they left the field. Eventually, Russell Hall came to pick him up and take him to the doctor. Russell Fowler lived at Mingoose and had to walk or cycle to and from the game – and afterwards walk to Redruth for an evening out.

The following is a list of players during the early 1940s:
Tommy Curtis (Goalie/Right Back), Bill Cheshire (Goalie), Alfie Kneebone (Back), Jack Pascoe (Right Half), Johnny Williamson (Centre Half), Russell Fowler (Left Half), Charlie Tamblyn (Inside Right), John Barker (Outside Right), Charlie Gay (Inside Left), Peter Trebilcock (Inside Left), Richie Sandercock (Outside Left), Tony Dark, John Stafieri, Courtney Jenkin, Hugh George, Dinkie Stephens, Jacko Stephens, Chick Edwards, John Wilson, Clifford Holbeche, ? Taylor, Derek Mitchell, Donald Mitchell. With apologies to anyone whose name has been missed.

The medal below was presented to Russell Fowler but unfortunately he cannot remember to which competition it relates so if anyone can help then please let him know.

Ken Miners recalls an, "almost fight" between one of the visiting players, Raymond Kent, and spectators Stanley Ennor, Joe Tamblyn and Jack Roberts who were continually goading him. Stanley having one leg, Joe having one arm and Jack being able to run quite fast, it was resolved without a blow being thrown.

After the 2nd World War efforts were being made to restart the local teams and an amalgamation of St. Agnes and Mithian was proposed. The Mithian team met Dick and Leich Whitford of St. Agnes in the Mithian W.I. hall to discuss the proposal and agreement was reached with only one dissenting voice. That agreement signalled the end of Mithian Football Club.

Cricket

George Symmons recalls cricket being played in the 1940s and 1950s in the field on the left immediately before Mithian School when travelling from

St. Agnes. Ted Snell was a member of the Mithian team when they bowled out the entire St. Agnes team for one run. (I've never seen that mentioned in any of the numerous books on St. Agnes!)

The Mithian Cricket Club (MCC) was resurrected in the mid 1980s by Graham Dodd and others and developed into a splendid sporting and social group. Graham referred to the generous help given by Dave Kench of St. Agnes in supplying the necessary equipment. Regular fixtures included Truro Solicitors and the Trevaunance Point Hotel for which the Trevaunance cup was competed.

The home games were played in John Thorley's field at Mithian Downs moving, a few years later, to one of Ken Miner's fields. The quality of the pitch was a continual problem despite supreme efforts with the roller and a wide-tyred car! The venue eventually moved to Goonhavern but the remoteness from Mithian, and the decline in interest, marked the end of the activities of the club.

The club still exists in name and is one of the organisations providing a representative to the Village Association.

The Manor of Mithian

Hals refers to it as *"the Manor of Mythi-an i.e. Of Whey, a notable grange for Cows and Milk, (otherwise, if the Name be compounded of My-thyan (Saxon) my servant, or villain by inheritance was formerly the Lands of Winslade of Tregorick in Pelynt; an Hereditary Esquire of the White Spur, who forfeited the same, with much other land, by attainder of Treason, Tempore EDVARD VI. So that he himself or Queen Mary gave these Lands to Sir Reginald Mohun of Hall .... In this Manor is an ancient Free-chappel, now converted to a Dwelling-house wherein GOD was duly worshipped in former Ages by the Tenants thereof."* The reference to the chapel gives us no clue as to whether it was in the actual manor house or elsewhere on the estate.

As I have said in an earlier chapter, the Count of Mortain owned Tywarnhayle Manor but this must have been prior to Mithian Manor being created. Mithian Manor is said to have belonged to a French Nobleman prior to the Wynslade family and that seems perfectly reasonable considering the Norman French influence after 1066. There is reference to a an agreement involving a John Le Brett of Boscun but it has not been possible to make a positive connection with the Manor. The agreement said, *"......... to William her 1st born £10 to be pd at his pleasure if she did cut wood at Mythian woods. Edward III. Signed at Mythian."* (Edward III reigned from 1327 to 1377).

John Wynslade (various spellings) was married to Jane who was the daughter of Sir John Trelawney**.** Mithian Manor was in his family's ownership for many years before 1549 but he preferred to live in his Manor at Pelynt. He was executed as a traitor after his involvement in the Prayer Book Rebellion (or Cornish Commotion) of that year. He was one of the leaders of those who took up arms to fight for the continued use of Latin and against the imposed use of English in church services. He was found guilty and hanged, drawn and quartered at Tyburn in 1550.

His son, William, lived at Mithian Manor and was also involved in the uprising but he avoided execution. In, "A History of Cornwall" by F E Halliday, it says that William Winslade was .. *"... an impoverished Catholic exile, led a walking life with his harp to gentlemen's houses, wherethrough, and by his other qualities, he was entitled Sir Tristram; ...."* The manor and lands at Mithian were confiscated by Edward VI and given to the Mohun family.

It is, perhaps, ironic that we now celebrate in song a threatened rebellion in defence of Bishop Jonathan Trelawney and ignore this actual uprising that changed Cornish history and cost so many lives.

The Mohun family was given the Manor (together with Tregarrick at Pelynt) in the early 1550s, shortly after it was confiscated from the Wynslades.

It was actually given to Reginald (Reynold) Mohun by Edward VI and he bequeathed it to his son, William Mohun who lived there with his wife, Elizabeth. He became Sheriff of Cornwall a few years later.

William Mohun (probably Sir William's second son) was involved in defending Cornwall against the Spanish Armada in the 1580s and on the death of his father in 1588 he assumed ownership of the Manor. During the early 1630s to the early 1680s Nathaniel Mohun was Lord of the Manor and was followed by his son, William. Lord (Warrick) Mohun of Boconnoc succeeded him and it was he that maintained detailed accounts and records which provide a good picture of the estate in the early 1700s. The Mohuns were very active in supporting King Charles before and during the Civil War in the 1640s. It is said that they had a tendency to delay giving support until they could see which side was winning and it looks as though they got it disastrously wrong on this occasion. Lord Mohun resigned his commission in September 1643 and surrendered to Fairfax when Cornwall yielded in 1646. The Civil war and interregnum lasted from 1642 to 1660 and there is no evidence of any fighting in or around Mithian. Without doubt , however, individuals from Mithian would have been involved in the many battles and skirmishes across Cornwall and it is quite possible that the Mohun family would have expected their tenants to join their regiment on the side of the King.

There is reference to a lease in the 1650s between the Mohuns and the Ennors for the Grist Corn Mill involving a John Cleather of St. Agnes. In 1677 another lease was drawn up between the same parties for Mill Pool and tenement although I am not sure if this relates to the property now known as Mill Pool or to the Grist Mill.

From the Court Rolls Hugh Tonkin is named as a Free Tenant and the following as Conventionary Tenants; M Crocker (gent), M Hawkyn, John Enner, John Bowallack, James Enner, Barkle (later Barkla), Borlase, Billing, Paull, Nancarrow, Morrish, Hodge, Chenoweth and others totalling up to 40.

The Mohun's involvement with Mithian finally came to an end and a monument at St.Ewe reads *"Here lyes the Body of Willian Mohun.Esq., the last of that Ancient Name and Noble family. He died December the second, 1737; aged 32. This monument was erected by his Widow, Sibella Mohun, Sister of Thomas Trefusis, of Penryn, Esq., and his only sister,*

Elizabeth Prowse, widow of James Prowse, of Keyford in the County of Somerset, Esq., in gratitude to his memory."

The Mohun family had owned the Manor for over 200 years and its disposal is described in Lakes "Parochial History of Cornwall" where it states that Wm Mohun *"bequeathed it to his wife Sibella, (who afterwards married John Derbyshire Birkhead esq.), and his sister, Mrs Elizabeth Prowse. Sir Christopher Hawkins, bart., bought it in 1777; one moiety of Mr Birkhead and the other of Matthew Grylls, brother and heir of Robert Grylls, who had purchased it in 1758 of the devisees of Mrs Prowse. It is now* (1867) *the property of the Messrs Richard and Horton Davy, who inherit it from their father the late Stephen Davy Esq."*

Sir Richard Vyvyan is said to have been the Squire and Lord of the Manor of Mithian in 1780 but whether this is at variance or in concurrence with the above I am not sure. (The Vyvyan family certainly owned the lands to the east of Mithian River). The landowners were said to be John & Ann Hawkins, Christopher Hawkins, Gilbert Hele Chilcott and Mary Veaile.

In the 1842 Manor Tithe for Mithian the following statistics are shown;

Arable Land	3,872 acres
Meadow or Pasture	100 acres
Waste Commonland and uncultivated Land	2685 acres
Total	6657 acres

Wheat	7s 0¼d	per bushel
Barley	3s 11½d	per bushel
Oats	2s 9d	per bushel

An entry in the Gazetteer of Cornwall in 1884 states that it is, *"A manor belonging to Mrs J M Williams and Mr R Davey, comprising 170 small tenements inclosed from a common, chiefly within the last 40 years. Contents about 1000 acres."* Mrs Maria Williams was a widow and a sister of William Horton Davey. Richard Davey died in June 1884 and his nephew, Joshua Sidney Davey, inherited his estate.

In 1900 the Manor of Mithian was sold and became part of the estate of the Williams of Caerhays Castle but they are not thought to have had any presence in the village.

The Cornwall County Council Monuments Records state that it is, *"Now converted into five dwellings. The conversion has effectively hidden the lines of the old manor but there is still a fine plaster ceiling that has been divided by a partition wall. In another cottage is a fine old staircase. The date of the original building and the conversion are unknown."*

M H Bizley's book, "Friendly Retreat" provides some interesting facts about the Manor including details of various leases and Court Records.

Mithian Manor Chapel

There are many references to a chapel in the centre of the village but its exact location seems to have been lost in the mists of time. Considering the many references to it, I believe that it did exist and some of the articles are included to enable you to form your own conclusion. If you have any further information, or would like to investigate it further, then please let me know.

Lake's Parochial History and W. Hals recorded a free chapel at Mithian, as having been converted to a dwelling house, *"wherein God was worshipped in former ages by the tenants thereof..."* This does not seem to have been well regarded by some later writers as they have suggested that the chapel was a fiction, although W Penaluna wrote of the chapel in 1838. There certainly seems to be no written documents of any chapel and the building seems to have totally vanished. There is not even a local tradition of a chapel. The CCC Monuments Records state, "*Although OS could find no information about the chapel, local tradition locates it close to Mithian Farm, and with a graveyard, and also speaks of a monastery here.*"

Courtney Jenkin, who lives in Mithian farm, is convinced that there was a monastic chapel located in one of the farm buildings and that the graveyard is located nearby.

It is also suggested that the chapel was a part of the manor house itself and the rear elevation and the existence of a room that could have been for such a purpose, does support this.

An entry in, "A Study of Celtic Hagiology" refers to an, "*Ancient chapel at Mithian as late as the middle of the 18th century, remains of it were standing in 1843, but it seems to have been entirely demolished by 1847. .... This was the chapel of the Mithian estate and the successor of a Celtic Oratory, perhaps of St Mevanu.."* St Mevanus or Meen could have been the Patron Saint of Mithian.

Hals, in discussing the presence of a free chapel in the Manor, says, "*Now libera Capella, according to the Canonists, is a Chappel, by the Licence of the King, founded and envowed by the Bounty of well-disposed Christians with Lands, Contributions, or Compositions, for their private*

Ease and Convenience in serving GOD near their own Homes, without being obliged to go far off to the Parochial or Mother Church; and such are called free Chapels in respect of their being exempt from the Diocesan Bishop's Visitation, and founded, as aforesaid, by Licence of the King of England, or Duke of Cornwall in those parts."

A report of 1820 makes reference to a Free Chapel and in the tything of 1842 there is mention of Church Lane which may relate to the field called Park-an-Eglos. Two small pieces of pottery were recently found in this field and they have been identified by the Royal Cornwall Museum as Lostwithiel Ware from the 15th, or more probably, the 16th or 17th century. Nothing very remarkable about this but Graham Dodd and I were actually examining the area to try and find something that may have suggested the existence of a building – maybe even a chapel.

Mining and Agriculture

I have included this section because this village depended heavily on both of these industries for employment. Both involved very hard work in harsh conditions and employment in them meant that there was little time for anything else. Wages were low but at least some money was coming into the house. There was, however, little opportunity to improve the lot of your family.

That Mithian was very dependent on mining is not in doubt but many authoritative books cover this industry much better than I can and I have given it only a superficial mention here.

Located at Wheal Davy farm are WHEAL BUTSON and WHEAL BURROW that were within the Manor of Mithian. A K Hamilton Jenkin states that they were first mentioned in 1735 under the name of WHEAL DAVEY but he also says that Wheal Butson and Wheal Davey were almost identical so this does seem a little confusing.

Also referred to are two mines a little further down the Trevellas valley, *"Northward, down the valley, where the Trevellas stream is now spanned by the viaduct of the Truro to Newquay branch line, stands WHEAL LIBERTY and WHEAL VALLEY, small mines that have nonetheless*

been tried on a number of occasions. Wheal Valley lies for the most part on the west bank of the coombe, and Liberty on the east; but it is clear that the workings of each mine extended beneath the valley bottom from one side to the other." It seems that Wheal Liberty closed as early as 1840. Yet another Knackt or Scat bal as disused mines are referred to in Cornwall.

Wheal Mithian has been described as unidentifiable but is said to be 1,000 feet to the southeast of the village. The Ordnance Survey map shows a shaft in a field just below the chapel and there is evidence of mining activity further up the hill behind Rose Merryn. There is also reference to a Wheal Albion near-by so the picture is not clear. An advertisement in the Cornwall Gazette dated 3rd August 1805 advertised shares in Wheal Mithian for sale. Wheal Goshen is near to Goshen Farm and, although no shafts are shown on the map, there is ample evidence of overburden. The area around Montrose Farm seems to be within the Prince Royal or Princess Royal mine area.

Hamilton Jenkin also refers to Captain Oates of Rose-in-Vale who reputedly profited by £30,000 in the 1830s from the, "Navvy Pit" surface mine near Porthtowan. This was probably so named because navvies were used to dig rather than the higher paid miners.

Many taverns sprung up to serve the mining community and concern was expressed in Parliament that miners were becoming very reliant on them. The practice of workers having to draw their wages in cash from these alehouses on condition that one shilling (5P) in the pound was spent there was of particular concern. It was felt that having spent the obligatory amount they would be unlikely to stop until they were intoxicated. There was also the practice of miners being paid with tokens that had to be spent in certain shops that were probably run by the mine owners.

Halvaners made a living by extracting any remaining tin from mine burrows, employing mostly youngsters to carry out the task. Considering the number of, "knackt bals" in the area there must have been a lot of scope for them.

Although Cornish mining continued into the 20th century it was only a few mines that kept it alive. There are many 19th century reports that talk of the disaster hitting Cornwall both from the financial and the human aspect. Many of the mining speculators came from outside the county and there is one report in the 1880s that states that, "Cornish gentlemen would never have touched it with a pair of tongs."

Like so many Cornish communities, the St. Agnes area was hit hard by the huge migration of workers during the 19th century. With the closing of so many mines attempts were made to provide alternative employment and work that could have been undertaken by horse and implement was often carried out manually. Commendable as this was, there was a limit to how far it could be taken. With little alternative work, there was no option for many but to move to the "new" mining areas of the World. There is reference elsewhere in this book to families being involved in the large migration but these were the mining captains who could afford to return. For the ordinary miner and his immediate family it was often a one-way ticket with the likelihood that they would not see their remaining family again. Stories abound of long lost relatives being traced to Australia, America, South Africa etc and there is one from my own family that is particularly poignant. A family of four boys approached their parents to say that they wanted to emigrate to the USA to find mining work. The parents were devastated as they knew that they may never see them again. Reluctantly they agreed that the three eldest could go but that the youngest, still a teenager, should stay behind. He was, however, allowed to travel to Southampton with his brothers to see them on their way. In a move that seems unlikely to have been spontaneous, he joined them on the ship and sailed away to America. It is not difficult to imagine the desolation suffered by the parents when he failed to return.

Cornish communities were beginning to spring up around the world and I have read a number of references to postcards being sent home addressed to, "Cornwall, near England."

It is said that the Cornish pasty was invented for the miners who would carry them underground for their croust. This may well be the case but there is a lot of nonsense talked about them. I've heard of compartmentalised pasties containing both sweet and savoury sections, ingredients that include carrots and all sorts of other trade, being able to drop one down a mine shaft and the pastry not break and even that you should hold the crimping and eat the pasty along its side. Far be it from me to tell a Cornish lady how to bake a pasty but I do know that it should have potato, onion, swede and pasty meat, the pastry should melt in your mouth, the gravy run down your cheeks and that you should eat it from the end, preferably out of a paper bag.

Anyway, it is important to always leave a corner for the Knockers or Knackers. These are little people who live in the mines and, as thanks for the tasty titbit, they keep you safe from harm. Needless to say, they should not be confused with fairies, sprites, leprechauns etc. which are all mythical.

Many villagers were involved in agriculture either as tenants, landowners or labourers. Examination of the Tythe map of 1840 shows that there were many tenant farmers in Mithian, some of whom held just a few fields. In contrast, there were two major holdings in the village. James Ennor rented Trewartha or Warra Farm and, apart from including some fields that were remote from the unit, is in the area of the existing holding. It also included the gristmill and homestead near the Rose-in-Vale. John Woolcock farmed what we now know as Mithian Farm but it is interesting to note that there were a number of minor holdings within his notional boundary. The owners of most of the property and land in Mithian were Stephen and Richard Davey and you will have seen reference to this family with regard to ownership of Mithian Manor. There are two fields between Trewartha Farm and the main St. Agnes to Perranporth road that were not let but were retained by the Daveys for their own use. Other minor tenants included William Blight, William Dunstone, John Borlase, James Roberts, Isaac George, James Letcher, William Mitchell, Ralph Houghton, Mary Butson and William Tremewan.

John Eley recalls, "Hand Mows" being built in the fields in the1950s, perhaps to aid drying or to avoid using the valuable dry weather in carrying the corn. Six shocks of seven sheaves would be arranged into the shape of an inverted cone. The top layer being placed with the corn heads facing down to aid drainage. This could be safely left for a few months until there was time available to build the rick.

"Hand Mows" with Mithian Church in the background. Photo by Ken Young.

Harvest was a busy time of the year and the following description relates to the process in the 1950s and 1960s at Wheal Davy farm where my wife grew up.

The produce was cut and bound into sheaves by the binder and these were assembled in shocks where they dried before being transported to the site where the rick was to be built. Jack Roberts was fastidious in his rick building and the thatching and alignment of ropes seemed as important for appearance as for protection.

Threshing (pronounced thrashing) was carried out during January to March when stocks of corn and straw were getting low. The process of threshing had not changed much over the years except that the source of power for the machinery had changed from steam engine to diesel (or TVO) tractor. Jack used a local contractor, Jennings of Anchor Farm, Trevellas and later, Desmond Carlyon of Redruth, to undertake this and they would fit it in with the work that they had to do for other local farmers. The process of separating the cereal from the straw was very hard and dusty work but it still evokes pleasant memories amongst (some) those who were involved.

Gwen had the task of keeping the workers fed and watered and mid-morning croust always consisted of saffron or yeast buns and a cup or two of tea. A couple of hours later would see everyone sitting down for dinner (or lunch if you prefer) that would consist of tiddy and turnip pie, under-roast (always with a roll of pastry on the side) or pasty (potato, turnip, onion and pasty meat in a pastry covering which was crimped on one side). This was invariably followed by rice pudding. Of course, if pasties were being served then the tea would be sugary. Sue says that she well remembers one of the helpers, Hartley Stevens, politely explaining that he would have to leave the table and go outside to remove a mouse from his trouser leg.

A few years later the threshing sets and binders were replaced by combine harvesters and bailers. Instead of the harvest being cut in summer and threshed in winter it had become a completely summer job with the cereal and straw being stored quite separately. Jack had his own Combine Harvester but also called in John Mitchell from Trewartha to help out. During my summer holidays I worked on a nearby farm and my first job was to ride the combine harvester and bag the corn. It was extremely dusty and I soon generously volunteered to walk and load the straw and let someone a little older have the riding job!

Gwen's job also changed slightly in that summer refreshments were required for the long summer days when work could, and would, run on into the late evenings. Afternoon tea was now on the menu and this consisted of sandwiches, scones or splits with jam and cream (applied in that order!) and large enamel jugs of tea. Of course, the sun always shone and the prevailing memory is of sitting on a bail of straw with the dog at your feet waiting for his share of the delicacies.

Compared to just a few years ago there is now very little agricultural activity in Mithian and the days of the homestead with a few acres are long since gone.

This 1950s picture shows Major doing the hard work whilst being led by Courtney Jenkin with Jack James handling the plough. The location is the rear of Underwood and Mrs. Elsie Bricknell and Mrs. Edwin Brokenshire are the spectators.

Recollections

This section contains snippets of both happy and sad events and I hope that some of the items will evoke memories of the village you remember or have been told about. I hope that you will indulge me by allowing me to stray slightly to talk about my own boyhood during the 1950s. Not in Mithian, I concede, but in neighbouring Silverwell, a much more disparate village but in many other respects, very similar to Mithian.

At the age of five, in 1951, my family made the move from Looe to settle in Silverwell and it was here that I was to spend my next nineteen years before my marriage in 1970. My father worked for Mr. and Mrs. Noel Hoskins at Greenacre Farm. A good farmer and a good friend. We lived in Lilac Cottage (Pump Cottage) which was tied to the farm. As I mentioned earlier, Silverwell is very spread out and, unlike Mithian, has no discernable centre. I recall mains water supply being installed where previously we used a hand pump that had to be primed with water left from the previous pumping session. Failure to save enough meant a long walk to the river to fetch a bucket of water. I remember the taste of the water as being slightly metallic and very, very cold.

Prior to mains electricity we relied on candles and oil lamps and anyone who has used the Tilley lamps will recall the fragile, white mantles that glowed to provide the brilliant light although this was very dim compared to even a 40 Watt bulb. The purchase of an engine with a generator meant that convenience lighting had arrived and the 12 Volt supply seemed like heaven especially as we were able to run a small television albeit with a rolling, flickering screen that would be switched off in disgust these days. From our mark 1 generator we progressed to a startamatic and if I remember correctly, it would burst into life when an electrical switch was turned on.

Our house had a large kitchen with a Cornish range and it was, occasionally, my job to clean it. This was not the most pleasant job as the black bits needed blackening and the brass bits polishing. In spite of the mess that I always made I was still enlisted to take my turn. For smaller cooking jobs the primus stove was used and I suppose that it can be compared with the modern day microwave oven.

Our lavatory was located in the rear garden and was a very old stone building with a slate roof. It was not a place to linger due to the abundance of wildlife there; the certain presence of spiders and the lack of light ensured that it was always a quick visit. After a while a cesspit was installed but prior to that it was a case of bucket and chuck it.

Both Mithian and Silverwell were heavily reliant on agriculture and the sounds and smells of farming were almost always present. In those days the aroma of silage and dung seemed natural and somehow less objectionable. My father milked the cows and I would love to watch although this was always in the afternoons, as I didn't like the early mornings. The clanging of the metal churns is a memory that does not fade. They were filled, loaded into the transport box and taken down the lane to the milk stand to await the lorry. I recall the early 1950s when Shire Horses were still in use and, at the age of five, being placed on one. It was like sitting on top of a mountain and was not an experience I enjoyed.

During school holidays and weekends I fed and mucked out the pigs. At that time, they were housed in a variety of sheds located around the yard, all having access to a field. I also helped with the harvest but I do not recall this with the feeling of nostalgia that I often read about. It was very hard work and after the first day my muscles ached so bad that my parents had to nag me to get up from my bed the following morning.

So much of what we did seemed to revolve around the chapel. There were the annual occasions; Tea Treat, Harvest Festival and Anniversary when all of the children had to sing or recite. My singing was not considered very angelic so it was the recitation for me. I remember that some children attended from Mithian, in particular that Suzanne Roberts. Her rendition was always word perfect and about five times longer than mine and I remember thinking that no one likes a smart-ass; but they did!

Silverwell has a story of its own and it is not the subject of this book but I believe that growing up in the two villages would not have been that dissimilar; playing in the streams, in the woods and nicking other people's apples. I hope, therefore, that you will forgive this short digression and that you may even have recognised in it a little of Mithian life.

The Cornwall Gazette reported a sad event in 1854 when it announced the death of an 11-year old boy. James Christopher was killed after being kicked in the head by a colt and, at the subsequent inquest at the Miners Inn, a verdict of accidental death was brought in.

The Cook Family lived in the village and was the victim of an agricultural practice that would horrify us today. A report in the Royal Cornwall Gazette on 24th July 1863 describes a case brought before the Truro Board of Guardians for alleged nuisance that, "it was supposed, had been the cause of disease and death in that neighbourhood." It appeared that Mr. Hall, the Inspector of Nuisances, had received an anonymous communication via the police. It referred to a young family called Cook who lived in a house adjoining the old farm-house formerly occupied by Mr. Woolcock and

where he stored dead horses, cows and sheep where they would rot for manure.
It was reported, *"The smell was offensive to the whole village so it must have been dreadful for the Cook family who, whilst sleeping, inhale the poison with their every breath. Mr Hall found a covered pit and, after removing the covering, ran out of the building saying he would not return for payment of £500. He visited it again the following week and found that the Cook family were better, that the children had been removed and that none of the family had died. After further remarks and discussion the subject dropped."*

In August 1906 a fire gutted a cottage at Whitestreet Farm (Sandow's cottage). The damaged buildings were repaired and used as a farm building and a new dwelling was built close by. The Royal Cornwall Gazette carried the following report of the event, *"Mr Harry Sandow of White-street met with a severe misfortune on Thursday night when his dwelling-house was burnt to the ground. Some neighbours discovered the fire (which attacked the rear of the house and roof), and were able to save the furniture, besides removing the stairs and the windows from the burning building."* It seems dangerous to the point of being foolhardy to risk removing these items whilst the fire was raging but when it is considered that they were probably the most expensive elements of the dwelling and that there was probably no insurance cover, you begin to understand why the risk was taken. The new dwelling was the home of my wife's mother prior to her marriage in 1935 and it is now occupied by Ken and Margaret Adams.

I remember Jack Roberts telling me about a young boy in Mithian who was accidentally killed by his father with a pick. The father was using the pick to dig a hole and the toddler walked around the back of him as he swung it over his shoulder. A tragic accident and we can only imagine the feelings of the father.

There was a time when animals were driven (walked) to market and Irven Solway and his brother, who were aged twelve and eleven, were given the task of walking three bullocks to Truro Cattle Market sometime around 1910. Unfortunately they failed to sell and they had to walk them home again.

Jack King's brother was tragically and mysteriously killed during the early 1900s when he fell down a well adjacent to the Hermitage. Up until that time there had been a hand-pump installed there but this was then removed and a more permanent cover provided to the well.

Franklyn Ennor had many old stories and one of these involved an old farmer who lived in Mithian Woods, across the valley from Goverley, Mithian Downs. The house and buildings have long been derelict but the story endures. Tired of trying to find a stick to stir the pig swill he suddenly realised that he always had one available and, from then on, took to using his wooden leg. The story could well have been the origin of the old Cornish saying, "If you don't schemey then you gotta louster."

There was always a great deal of rivalry between the gardeners of the village with many claims and counter claims regarding the size and quality of the produce. On one occasion an argument broke out about the size of a flatpoll cabbage that had been brought into the pub. Bill Brown said that he had one at home bigger than the specimen on the bar and he was challenged to "prove it." He promptly went to the other man's garden, where Kando Cottage now stands, and cut the biggest one he could find. On comparing the two it was adjudged that Browney's was the larger after which he took it back and placed it back on the stump. On another occasion he cut the stump twice so that it could not be proved from where the cabbage had been cut.

Children can be very cruel as I am sure Mr. Rogers, the cobbler, thought when they crept into his cobblers shop and replaced his pet canary with a crow. Or when he discovered that the lads from the village had tied a rope around his cobbler's shop and tried to pull it into the road.

This picture shows Sunny Villa prior to 1914 when it was destroyed when a firework set the thatched roof alight. The fire brigade was not as efficient as it is today and the cottage was completely gutted. James George Brewer, (Perranporth haulier) bought it as a shell and rebuilt it in a style that did not exactly fit in with the rest of the village. Local Authority planning was not as influential as it is today although it could be argued that the consistency of more recent approvals do not advance that argument; but we won't go there!

Charlie Mora remembers the early 1920s when the children of the village were allowed to ride on the hay wagons at harvest time. In this he remembers Beryl Brown in particular but I did not press him as to why. He also remembers looking forward to being sent up to Trewartha Farm to fetch the milk as Mr. Woolcock would usually give him a scoop of clotted cream off the top of the milk.

Joe Tamblyn lost an arm when it became tangled in the chaff cutter pulled by a horse whim during the 1920s. A common type of accident in those days when safety guards were not required by law. This did not stop him working however and he could often be seen wheeling a barrow supporting one side with his arm and the other by a length of rope passing over his shoulder.

Sometime in the 1920s, Franklyn Ennor's brother, was drowned in Jericho Valley when he walked into the bushes to take a closer look at a blackbird and fell into the flooded mine workings. His body was recovered with some difficulty and the entrance bricked up.

Bill Brown (Browny)

Joe Tamblyn was very keen on football and young lads from the period remember him bringing a wireless to Mithian School so that the children could hear King George V open the Wembley Football Exhibition.

I've mentioned elsewhere that rabbit was a part of the staple diet and Ken Miners recalls one particular family being raised almost entirely on rabbit, potatoes and salted fish. There was real poverty then and families were quite prepared to turn to cheap or free meals.

Franklyn Ennor worked in the mine at Jericho for a period and one of his jobs was to dispose of the hot ash from the steam engine that drove the pump. He was probably thinking more about the chapel or football or maybe why his pipe would not light, when he absentmindedly shovelled the hot ash into his wooden barrow. It caught alight very quickly and his load fell through the hole in the bottom. The story and leg pulling that followed took a little longer to go away.

Many simple games were played by the children of a few years ago. Games that had existed for generations and did not need organising; they just happened. Games like the, "Kissing Ring", "Rounders"(the game that is still played), "Twos and Threes" and "Duff in the Back" (a person runs around a circle of people and taps one person on the back. The giver and receiver of the blow then run in different directions around the outside of the circle in an attempt to occupy the single vacant space). In his paper, John King suggests these games were often the starting point of many a romance." I would add to this the game of winking that we always seemed to play at Sunday school events. This involved the girls sitting in a circle with a boy behind each one but with one empty chair. The boy behind the vacant chair winks at one of the girls and she has to make a dash for his chair. The boy behind her also has to watch for the wink as it is his job to try and restrain her. It seemed great fun to us and involved many a complaint regarding the means of restraint.

Ken Benney recalls a traction engine on a low loader coming to grief on Chapel Hill during the 1930s. The vehicle had taken a wrong turn at Mithian Downs and had carried on oblivious to the road layout around Mithian. The traction engine toppled off the lorry and fell against the hedge where it lay for some time before it was hauled upright and loaded back onto the lorry, an event that must have generated a lot of interest to the children and a talking point for the old timers of the village.

William (Billie) Gilbert lived with his grandfather, Isaac Gilbert near the Wheal Butson railway bridge. In July 1935 he was travelling to Perranporth on his bicycle and the brakes failed on St.George's Hill. Unable to stop or control the bike he careered down the hill and was killed.

Freda Male née Crebo recalls enjoying her time at Mithian School but not being too keen on school life after transferring to St. Agnes. It was a long walk to St. Agnes and rainy days were always welcome when they would roll in the puddles and be sent home for being wet.

Stanley Harris worked as a paperboy for Miss O'Leary for which he was paid 2/6 (12.5p) per week. This did not seem enough to Stanley's friends and he was talked into asking for more money. Encouraged by them, he told her that she should give him a rise in pay. She explained that she could not afford to pay him any more and that there would be no pay rise. The friends then came up with the idea that he should tell her that he had been offered another job with more money. She responded that she had already found a replacement and that he could finish at the end of the week and poor Stanley was out of a job.

Ken Symmons recalls the 1930s and 1940s as being a time of mend and make do especially when his father asked him to carry out a few repair jobs around the house. Before refrigerators and freezers were the norm, external meat safes were used. These were cupboards with zinc gauze in the door to ventilate while keeping flies out. He was asked to make one using old lard boxes. When he complained and asked for some decent timber his father responded with, "Call yourself a carpenter." He also had to replace some rotten skirting with the same material but found that the wood was too greasy to paint. Theirs was the only house in Mithian with, "Pure Lard" stamped on their skirting.

Some of the things that the lads and, perhaps lasses, got up to sound particularly scary but "health and safety" hadn't been invented in those days. Like stuffing sacks down the chimney of the Men's Institute during a meeting whilst the fire was lit. Like tying dynamite to a cartwheel and rolling it down a hill. Like tipping over an outside toilet with "Flippa" Rogers still in it. Like encouraging a lad to saw off a branch of a tree and forgetting to mention that it was the one that he was sitting on. Like rolling a large tractor tyre down, "The Lane" and knocking over Mrs. Rice who lived in Rose-in-Vale cottage (Pat Ely's, née Brokenshire, excuse was, "We didn't think that it would go that far")

Although there was always lots of work to be done there was also time for relaxation. Mostly it involved impromptu activities when the villagers would get together for some sport either amongst each other or in competition with a neighbouring village. Greyhound or whippet racing was popular and easy to organise and, if you had a gun, then clay pigeon shooting provided good fun. Although money was not very plentiful, there always seemed to be some available for a small wager on the side. That gave the competition a bit more edge and although the winnings would probably disappear on the first round in the pub the win would be remembered and savoured for a long time.

Goodbodys of Plymouth were regular suppliers of pasties to George Symmons' shop and they were very popular. Mr. Mannell, who helped build the railway and who worked at Lambriggan mine, regularly bought one every weekday and two on Saturdays the extra one, presumably, being for Sunday. These sold at 4d each and it is to be hoped that Goodbody's suppliers were based in Cornwall.

George Symmons Snr. agreed to buy some packs of village photographs in 1937. The photographer duly set to work and produced a set of six views of the village. George thought that he had signed an order for six dozen packs that he proposed selling at a halfpenny each or 3d per pack. He had, unfortunately, signed for 60 boxes containing umpteen packs. He accepted it as his error and took delivery and boxes of the cards were stored all over the house. He despaired at ever being able to sell them and even resorted to using them as notepaper. When World War II started and personnel at RAF Perranporth from all over the world swelled the village population, they were in great demand and he was able to increase the price and sell the lot.

George Symmons Snr. decided that he would like to learn to play the accordion but despite his constant practice he still managed to make a dreadful din. His wife became exasperated at this and threatened to leave him if he didn't stop the noise. To overcome the problem he decided to inflict the pain on the neighbours by practising outside the shop front door. He could often be seen sitting there playing the instrument but despite his perseverance he never did master it.

Rabbits were caught by many people for home consumption and for selling through the local shops or to Tonkins of Truro. If they were to be sold to Tonkins then it was likely that they would be sent via the bus driver who would also collect payment for them. Before the motorised buses were used, it was a common sight to see the rabbits hung on the shafts of the horse bus so that the smell was kept outside the compartment. Bags of animal skins were also collected from the butcher, Tom Bartle, and taken to Truro. This must have been an unpleasant experience for the passengers on a hot day but it seems that people were less concerned about such smells in those days.

It was the task of one young girl to fetch the milk from Jimmy Rowe's farm and, being partial to a drink of milk, she would take a few mouthfuls from the jug and top it up from the standpipe just below the Men's Institute. It was not until her mother complained to Jimmy Rowe about the quality of the milk that her refreshment breaks were discovered.

Every schoolboy and some girls had a nickname; some less complimentary than others. Remembering or admitting to them can be a problem but Tommy Mitchell was always referred to as Tommy Treacle because of his passion for treacle sandwiches.

It seems that Foot and Mouth disease has always been with us and during the early 1940s it struck nearby. Four farms at Trevellas were affected and there were great fears that it would spread to neighbouring villages. Arthur Benney recalls that military machines from the aerodrome were used to dig large trenches where the animals were buried in lime. The limited outbreak was contained without too much expense or publicity and certainly without horrendous cremations.

Freda Male recalls growing up with many of the people named in this book and of being very close to Maurice Chapman who, "was like a brother to me." She recalls the two of them making blackberry pies in an old pigsty which they had cleaned out and in which they had installed a cooker. Apparently there were other children who wanted to share the "kitchen" but Maurice and Freda were not keen on this. Even at that young age, Maurice displayed his future business acumen by setting down on paper the terms and conditions for its use by others.

We now accept that the Cory bin lorry will arrive to remove our rubbish but this was once collected by Dick Harvey with his horse and cart and taken to Wheal Prudence, Cross Coombe, where it was dumped down the mineshaft. Unlike today, the amount collected was minimal; any food left over was fed to the animals and the few containers were all re-used. Ashes from the fire may have needed to be disposed of but even that was often tipped in a large pit where the contents of the privy would then be placed.

Another Tea Treat, this time in the field below Trewartha Farm and sometime during the late 1930s. The quality of the original is very poor but I have included it anyway.
Pictured from left to right are: Back row: Martha Rice, May Tippett, Bessie Lavin, Ereta Crebo, Alma Retallack, Frederica Miners. Front Row: Sidney Shugg, Alfred Hoskins, Franklyn Ennor and George Symmons Jnr.

"Chippy" Chapman from Roche worked in Mithian for the Brokenshires. His ambition was to drive a tractor and Jimmy Rowe and one or two of the other boys "kindly" offered to give him a lesson or two before he was allowed near a tractor. They took Chippy to Jack James' cowshed at the top of Chapel Hill, on the left, and gave him two milking stools; one to sit on and the other to act as a steering wheel. They issued the instructions to which Chippy dutifully changed gear, worked the brake and steered around a series of imaginary obstacles. Chippy thought that he was doing quite well and did not realise until later that he was providing the entertainment for all of the children of the village who were peering through the windows.

Arthur and Ken Benney remember looking down from their garden in The Terrace and seeing Mrs. Facey's chalet on fire. This was located where Kando cottage now stands. The fire was so extensive that she had to move out and live with her daughter Mrs. George William Symmons.

There were many orchards in the village and scrumping was a popular pastime. Many people would have happily given some apples if asked but there was extra excitement in helping yourself. On one occasion in the 1930s plans did go awry when Mr. & Mrs. Drew accosted some lads who they suspected of scrumping but then let them off through lack of evidence. Unfortunately one did not get away quite so lightly as he had dropped his newly acquired driving licence in the orchard as he made his getaway (name withheld to protect the guilty).

Ken Miners recalls an occasion when the children of the village were in trouble for making too much noise. The snow was covering the ground and the sleigh was taken out and they all headed for the steeply sloping field behind Rose Merryn. Gwen Gunn was positioned on the front of the sleigh with Ken Benney seated behind with his arms around her. Her screams could be heard all over the village and Ken, no doubt, simply said that he had to hold on to something.

David Docking purchased an old Turkish bayonet from a friend at Mithian School. This must have been quite a trophy but he had not thought where he could keep it. Fearing that his parents would confiscate it he hid it in the roof of the Miners Arms; a place he remembers as being like a labyrinth and full of wildlife. Many years after he had moved from Mithian he read a newspaper article saying that, whilst carrying out repairs, workmen had discovered a very old sword in the Miners Arms roof. There was much speculation as to how it got there but David did not reveal the secret - until now.

David Docking was a close friend of Frank Benney whose job it was to pump the chapel organ for the hymn singing. David would sneak in through the Sunday school and join him at the rear of the organ where they would be chatting so much that Frank would forget to start pumping for the next hymn. They would then hear the thump, thump, thump of Stanley Ennor's artificial leg as he came to check out the problem. That would be David's signal to scarper.

Billy Quick lodged in the village and worked for the council repairing the roads. Ken Benney was a schoolboy at the time and remembers often chatting to Billy on his way to and from school. On one occasion he shouted to him to attract his attention and then threw a very ripe tomato, hitting him full in the face. Ken ran home but within a short while there came the inevitable tap on the door. Percy Benney, Ken's father, answered the door to Billy who still had the evidence running down his face. Billy said, "Look what your boy has done" and Percy promised to take the necessary action. He told Ken that he shouldn't have done it but Ken says that the most memorable thing was his father trying to stifle a laugh.

Ken Symmons remembers fishing at Millpool with boyhood friends and of usually catching a few small trout. A net would be stretched across the mouth of the tunnel under the railway line and the fish driven into it. I guess that a few wet clothes would have been forgiven considering the reward.

Maurice Chapman must have had a fright in 1930 when he was helping Jack James with his hay harvest. The field was very steep and he must have failed to properly apply the handbrake on his Fergie (Ferguson) tractor. News travelled very quickly and retrieving it from the stream must have been a bit embarrassing for him. The bodywork of the tractor was badly damaged but Gordon Proctor, who was a panel beater at Teagle's, carried out an expert repair job.

Most families were involved in, "lamping" and rabbit always featured on the weekly family menu. On a good night, the rougher the weather the better, you could bring home thirty rabbits according to Ken Benney. The equipment needed was a motorbike battery in a wooden box and a lamp with a handle that was held in the middle of the field. The rabbits would become mesmerised by the light and the dogs would pounce for the kill. Although the bags of rabbits were dropped at convenient points for later collection, the load could become quite heavy. On one occasion Arthur, Ken's brother, became a bit fed up at always having to carry the rabbits and decided to take over the battery and lamp. He promptly jumped over a hedge, tripped and fell on the battery box and was laid low for some time.

This was a period when youngsters were able to occupy their spare time in simple pastimes. Making Bee-skips was an art and a useful activity that ended with a finished product. I have not attempted a step-by-step description of the process but it needed both Arthur Benney and Ken Miners to get me to this stage of understanding. Apparently it involved taking a thick bramble and trimming off the prickles. It was then bruised, split down the middle and bound around a bunch of wheat straw. This was used to build up the shape of a beehive into which the swarm of bees would be shaken. If you would like to have a go at making one yourself then I would suggest that you contact one of the above mentioned gentlemen rather than me.

Ken Miners recalls that there was always plenty to occupy their time, *"after chapel on Sundays a few of the boys would go to St. Agnes or*

Perranporth to chat with the girls. I remember Arthur Benney, Donald Thomas, Ken Rice my brother and myself cycling to nearby villages to take part in their sports, like sheaf pitching and tug-o-war." At this point Betty interrupted to say, *"We girls used to do that too."*

Mithian certainly had its fair share of tragedies as the Kellow family must have felt in the mid 1930s. Leo Thomas Kellow was killed in a road accident in Tregolls Road, Truro when the motorcycle he was riding was in collision with a horse and wagon.

Ken Benney has a residing memory of Granny Bartle who lived at Underwood, next to the Miners Arms. When paying the greengrocer or butcher she would raise her long, black skirt to retrieve her purse. From where, he was never quite sure.

The presence of the air force personnel during World War II must have changed the complexion of village life considerably and it probably did the commercial establishments no harm at all. A certain lady who was known for entertaining the troops during the war was "on duty" one dark night when Ken & Roy Miners were on their way home from Perranporth. Roy felt the need to relieve himself and was shocked to find that he had chosen the same piece of hedge as the couple. Ken said that Roy seemed the more surprised.

Electricity came to the village around 1944 and prior to that, houses were lit by oil lamps, candles or Calor gas. I'm sure that there are many of you who remember the "Famous Lamp," Tilley pressurised lanterns and table lamps with their fragile mantles.

Florrie & Freddie Brokenshire lived in Bakery Cottage but Freddie was killed on 19th September 1947 at the age off thirty-three in a tractor accident near Montrose Barn. An Italian ex Prisoner-of-War was riding in the trailer and managed to leap clear. The Brokenshires were living in a tied cottage and Florrie and her three children had to vacate it within three weeks of his death but luckily they were able to find a new home close by, in Manor Cottage.

This was a time when everything seemed to be of use to someone including the old and sick animals. These were bought by one of the large local farms and sold to zoos as animal feed ("zoo meat").

John Eley recalls a colleague and himself being sent to the backlets (fields behind the pub) to spread salt in an attempt to kill the stinging nettles. They loaded the trap but all of the horses were in use and they had to resort to pulling it themselves. On the return journey to Mithian farm they met a travelling salesman who, jokingly, threatened to report them to the horses' union at which point they let go of the trap and it careered down hill and hit George Symmon's wall. I wonder how many times since then that this particular wall has been hit by a vehicle.

One Sunday afternoon in the summer of 1948 Percy Benney, who lived in the Terrace, saw smoke coming out of the Hermitage and called to his sons, Arthur and Ken. They broke through the door and managed to rescue two cats and three budgerigars. The owners, Mr. and Mrs. Victor Anderson, were known to be on Perranporth beach and whilst attempts to rescue the furniture continued, Harry Thomas was called in with his loud-speaker van to broadcast an appeal for them. A sterling effort was made by the neighbours to clear the house but there was still one room left when the fire officer gave the order to evacuate. There was little more than the walls standing at the end of the day, the thatched roof and all the interior had been completely destroyed and the furniture spread over the neighbours' gardens. The Andersons moved to Perranwell and the house stood empty for about five years. When it was eventually rebuilt the roof was replaced with cedar shingles.

Heather Harvey remembers her Saturday evening trips to Truro picture house when the bus was always crammed full notwithstanding the laws on overloading mentioned elsewhere. She did not elaborate on her comment that, "squeezing in was half the fun of it!"

Frank Benney, a brother to Arthur and Ken, was a sergeant in the army based in Germany and was tragically drowned during the 1950s whilst trying to save a colleague. The funeral was held at St. Agnes Church and was attended by a detachment of the Grenadier Guards who provided the military salute. It is recalled that the cortege was so big that the rear element was still in Barkla Shop when the hearse had reached the Church.

Vinegar was bought from the pub and the Miner's Arms sold it at 5d a bottle during the 1950s. The customer supplied the bottle and it was filled from a barrel.

Prior to the days when televisions were in every house it was quite normal to visit friends and relations to watch your favourite programme and Alice Beringer (née Godfrey) and her brother, Ralph, were regular watchers of Six-five Special at Miss O' Leary's.

This picture is of four ladies picking strawberries but there does not seem to be much activity taking place. From left to right are Joey, Mrs Horn, Freda Boundy, Unknown and Bernice Kellow. The picture was taken at Millpool during the very early 1950s.

One of the regulars in the pub always tied his pony and trap to a nearby gate whilst he was having a beer. Knowing that he would be somewhat inebriated on leaving some boys decided to play a trick on him. Separating the pony & trap, they placed one either side of the gate pushing the shafts of the trap through the bars. They reconnected pony and trap and waited until he reappeared. It took him some time to figure out why the pony would not move.

On another occasion Jim Dymond had ridden his bicycle to the pub and, on leaving, managed to get his leg through the middle of the frame. It seems that there were many watching him trying to extricate himself but no one helping.

Harry Thomas was known for his radio business and also for the provision of a Public Address system at all sorts of events. No matter whether it was a Tea Treat, fete, Furry Dance or whatever Harry always seemed to be there playing his music and holding the microphone.

This photograph taken by Ken Young in the 1950s features a number of local men but no one is able to recall why it was taken. The man on the left of the line was not from Mithian but I think that he was called McGuigan. Next to him and from left to right: Ken Benney, John Strike, Maurice Chapman with sons Roger and Ian, Edwin Brokenshire, Percy Benney, Tom Dyer and a former evacuee who I think was called Norman Fowler. The cottage in the background with the corrugated metal roof was the home of Katie Biddick.

During the early 1960s Mithian was hit by the great freeze when snow and ice covered the ground for weeks. For some reason, Tom & Maggie Dyer were the only source of running water in the village and they supplied everyone with buckets of water throughout the freeze up.

During the early 1970s one of Geoff Hoblyn's bullocks fell down a well and the Fire Brigade had to be called. Whilst awaiting its arrival Arthur Benney lassoed the animal's horns and managed to keep it afloat. The fire officer considered that special apparatus was required but they managed to pull it out manually using the lasso. The bullock simply shook itself and carried on grazing.

During the early 1980s, to the delight of children and adults alike, the village awoke to a blanket of snow. It was sufficiently thick to prevent any movement of vehicles up or down the three hills that provide access to and exit from Mithian. Cut off from the outside world, a few people ventured out on foot to enjoy the beautiful scenes and atmosphere that such conditions bring. It is not known who threw the first snowball although accusations were made. Suddenly, it seemed that the entire village was involved in a huge battle with no discernible armies, everyone attacking everyone else. This continued for some time until, exhausted, everyone adjourned to the Miners Arms where Colin Gilham, who was the landlord at the time, served up hot soup. A memorable day.

We normally associate air raid sirens with wartime and it came as a surprise to me that Mr. Targett of The Olde Forge was asked to be the holder of the local air raid siren in the 1980s. This was a portable unit but it required special wiring and apparatus within the house. It was withdrawn in the mid 1990s, the equipment removed and the paperwork lodged with the St. Agnes Museum.

Christmas Eve was an occasion when many would gather at the Miners Arms. With presents wrapped and food prepared it was a time to unwind and sing a few carols and songs with friends. The songs chosen were any of which the words could be remembered; Cornish, Irish, Australian and even English. For those that ventured out to the pub on New Year's Eve it was more of the same with the additional feature of fancy dress. The singing was never of a truly high standard but the enthusiasm was tremendous as we sang the traditional Cornish songs of Lamorna, The White Rose and, with appropriate reverence, Trelawney.

I visited Irven Solway to collect stories about his grandfather who lived in the Manor complex around 1900. Sadly, following a fall, he has since died but it was clear that he enjoyed the chance to talk about the, "old days" and to tell a few stories which I will repeat here.

Referring to Bobbie Mitchell who ran the bus service in Perranporth. Bobbie was talking to some, "up country" visitors and said that he recalled when there were only two houses in the main street at

Perranporth and he lived in the middle one. Irven didn't drink but recalled an old phrase that says that bread may be the staff of life but gin is life itself. He said that he couldn't write before he went to school and that hadn't changed much by the time he left, the only "O" level he had was the one in his spirit level. When Irven was aged 90 and his wife was 95 they attended hospital together. Irven was asked his age to which he replied, "I'm 90 years of age." The nurse then asked when he was born and his response was, "90 years ago." She then asked the age of his wife and Irven said 95. Any children? Enquired the nurse. "Not yet", said Irven.

Irven's hobbies were building clocks and model steam engines and many of the pieces were very impressive. He showed me a model static engine that could also run on compressed air. He said, "If you blaw in there you'll get 'n going." Despite having played in a brass band I had to, "give it up as a bad job." George Mitchell was there with us and solved the problem. He said to Irven, "You got the chap blowin' in the wrong hole!"

During the 1980s the village produced a newsheet entitled, "Mithian News & Views." I wrote the early editions with Barbara Gilman undertaking the compiling and typing and Chris Bones, the printing. David Chetwyn took over its production up to the time when he and his wife left the village.

An article appearing in the 10th edition (June 1986) written by the late Gladys Damsell and entitled, "Memories of Mithian" is repeated here. Gladys lived near Mithian for a number of years during the 1970s and 1980s and was a past President of Mithian Women's Institute.

"As I entered Rose-in-Vale Guest House (now Country Hotel) very recently for a function, as always it brought back many happy memories of the many times we stayed there for holidays before coming to Cornwall to live.

Mithian still holds the same attraction for me now, as it did then. Although it is not possible for me to attend all the functions that are held in the village, my absence is certainly not through lack of interest but just general circumstances.

Inevitably, through the years there have been changes in the village, but I feel that the alterations to existing properties and the new ones built have been carried out with thought and care and in keeping with the village generally.

I always think of Mithian as a village set in a green frame, i.e. the fields, trees and woods near and around – what better setting could any village have? It really is a beautiful spot.

Last but by no means least, the warmth of the welcome we received when we arrived for our holidays and also when we arrived in the village to make our home here – never once were we made to feel "furriners" and always, through the many years I have lived in the area I have felt the same warmth and friendliness.

Success to all the future hopes for the village – long may Mithian flourish."

Sonia (Polly) Fynn produced the front page cartoons or sketch each month and she has kindly agreed that some of them can be reproduced in this book. Her contribution to the monthly magazine was much appreciated and added a touch of professionalism to an otherwise amateur publication.

This cartoon related to the many properties used for summer let and which then stood empty for the remainder of the year. A copy was sent to David Penhaligon MP and a sympathetic reply was received but the problem still plagues many villages. There are a number of Polly's contributions spread throughout the book.

Events and Pastimes

Like most communities, Mithian celebrated the Silver Jubilee of Queen Elizabeth II on the 6th June 1977. There were traditional sports, games and entertainment followed by a tea for everyone.

The Golden Jubilee was an even bigger occasion when the road was closed and became the dining room for the villagers. There was a knobbly knees competition and other time honoured activities and everyone thoroughly enjoyed the occasion. Due to an oversight by the organising committee in not having invited the Queen and Prince Philip in time, they asked Betty and Ken Miners to be our own Royal family and very splendid they looked as the photograph shows. Ken seems to be listening to something interesting and I hope that his crown did not slip!

The Women's Institute was a splendid hall and a popular venue for concerts, whist drives and dances. Ken Benney remembers the village events that took place there and the dances that were always well supported. Its demolition was a sad loss to the community.

Probably the most ambitious, and the most successful village event was the open-air production of, "A Midsummer's Night Dream" at the Rose-in-Vale Hotel in the late 1980s. This was a Parent/Teachers presentation and Graham Dodd recalls that it took a lot of organising. A number of performances were presented during the course of a week featuring Tymescythe, a group from "up country" which included Alan and Sonia (Polly) Fynn and their two sons, Tom and Sam. It was an excellent production but not without risk and was underwritten by some of the members of the PTA. The costs amounted to about £5,000 but it did turn in a hefty profit. The costumes and lighting were hired from the Royal Shakespeare Company and had to be returned within a few days. Graham Dodd and Eric Morris drove a hired van to Oxford and all would have been well if Eric had not decided to refuel the vehicle by putting diesel into the coolant tank; an expensive mistake.

Freda Male recalls the Mithian Carnivals during the early 1930s. They were organised by the Women's Institute and the parade, led by a brass band, started from Tea Treat Field (Undertown) at Trewartha Farm. I have not been able to find any former carnival queens although Freda did achieve this honour at St. Agnes.

Duck Racing in Mithian River in the 1990s raised a lot of money but it rained, how it rained. There was a winner but nobody cared, everyone just wanted to get home to dry out.

Village Walks were a popular feature of the 1980s and 1990s and, because they were usually organised by Betty Miners, they were referred to as, "A Walk with Betty" and Sonia Fynn's cartoon captures the moment.

There was a particularly lengthy walk for the Golden Jubilee but by then, Betty had, "retired" and on this occasion Alan Price led the group.

I wonder how many can remember the village Pushball team which entered the Daily Mail national competition in the 1930s? There was stiff competition from neighbouring villages but I have not been able to find out who won the local heats. It involved a team of six players who had to push a 6'0" diameter inflated ball around a field in an attempt to score goals. Arthur Benney recalls that the team consisted of Harold Penrose, Nick Ennor, Percy Benney (Arthur and Ken's father), Tom Dyer, Charlie Toman and one other. The ball would be carried to the venue in Stanley Ennor's van but he cannot recall how it was inflated.

Horse Shows and Gymkhanas were a regular and popular feature in the 1920s and George Mitchell recalls them being being great fun and held somewhere near Mithian school.

Cornish Wrestling and boxing were very popular and Emery Croucher from Trevellas is remembered as being quite good at both. A temporary ring would be set up in the top corner of the "pub field" and the boys of the village would gather there for a few bouts. On one occasion Emery was boxing with Tommy Dyer and hit him a bit harder than intended, knocking him down. Tommy's brother, George, was upset at this and clambered into the ring to sort Emery out. Things didn't go quite as George had planned and the very next punch sent him to the canvas next to his brother. A few years later Emery had a metal plate fixed in his jaw and I imagine that brought his boxing career to an end. Emery worked for John Mitchell at Trewartha Farm where he met his wife. Later he had a butcher's round for many years and was also a proficient chiropractor.

Outings were arranged in the late 1980s and early 1990s and usually involved an evening trip to Porthleven or wherever, where good support was given to the local hostelry before stopping off for fish and chips on the return journey.

Keith and Margaret Eddy moved to the area in the 1980s and became very involved in village life. I well remember the events held at their home when the cost of the food and drinks always seemed more than the money taken but we always ended up making a profit. It may well have been creative accountancy but whatever was achieved on the financial side, they were excellent village "dos."

For a few years in the early 1980s, some enthusiastic carol singers toured the village accompanied by the unlikely combination of a flute and a Euphonium. I'm not sure if this was the forerunner of the annual Carol service that is now a firm fixture in the village programme but it was very enjoyable.

The Carol Service takes place in the village "square" although I do remember it being held in the chapel on one occasion, presumably because it was wet. Our stand-in compere decided to tell a joke which turned out to be not entirely suitable for the venue or the younger members of the gathered company. There were a number of people who were clearly offended but also, I like to think, many who were slightly amused by the situation that we found ourselves in. St Agnes band usually accompanied the singing and the service was never concluded without at least, one rendition of, "While Shepherds Watch" sung to the tune, "Lingham." The singing was interrupted by the arrival of Father Christmas on his sleigh (or in his car) and presents were distributed to the excited children before he continued on his way. Refreshments in the village hall (Men's Institute) completed the night, apart for those who rounded everything off with a visit to the Miners Arms.

With the ever increasing risk of litigation claims, making it necessary to pay hefty insurance premiums, it seems likely that village bonfire nights will die out and we will have to do something else to, "Remember the Fifth of November." For the moment, at least, they remain a very enjoyable aspect of the village programme. There has been the occasional problem like when the sparks from the fire were being blown towards some thatched cottages and we had to call out the fire brigade. It was not needed but it did add to the enjoyment when the children were given a guided tour of the machine.

In the 1930s Mithian had its own musical quartet providing entertainment at various venues. The singers shown in the photograph were Norman Rose, Leonard Tippett (tenor), Franklyn Ennor (base) and Hedley Roberts. The accompanying pianist was Connie Mitchell. Leonard Tippett was killed in a motorcycle accident in 1935 and John Salmon took his place. They were considered to be a fine quartet and even had the opportunity to make a recording but one of the four refused so it never happened.

Fund raising in Mithian is as much about enjoyment as making money and the annual, or more frequent, Cheese & Wine evening is very much a social occasion. Held in the village hall (Men's Institute) the attractive prices ensured that they were memorable (not so for some) nights. There is also the annual fete and the treasure hunt that do much for village life and for fund-raising.

The War years

All communities were affected by the 1st World War and village life had to adjust to some extent but people carried on as best they could and tried to put on a mask of normality. The war brought with it a lot of fear and concern of what might happen but the Sunday School Tea Treats and other events continued to take place and people went about their daily life.

The photograph records the 3rd D.C.L.I. recruiting march on the 20th May 1915 with a large crowd at Mithian being told that, "Your Country Needs You."

In 1918, the war ended in victory and peace celebrations took place in most communities. One such event was held in Mithian and was recorded in the Royal Cornwall Gazette on 6th August 1919, *"A large measure of success attended peace celebrations for Mithian ward on Saturday. Mr. John Tredinnick was the chairman of committees, Mr. F C Snell was secretary and Mr. John Berryman was treasurer. A service in the Council School was followed by a procession led by a brass band under the conductorship of Mr. H Robins."* The report went on to describe the sporting events and to list the winners of the races and the carnival. Two weeks later in the same newspaper it was reported that the event had raised £16 and that 2,000 people had attended.

With the advancement in aerial warfare World War II seemed much closer to home and the presence of Trevellas or Perranporth Aerodrome and the billeting of military personnel, was an ever-present reminder that we were on a war footing.

The nearby aerodrome was an important base and Frank Carpenter in his book, "St. Agnes 1001 – 1999" states, *"The airfield at Trevellas opened as R.A.F. Perranporth (even though most of the airfield was in the parish of St. Agnes). The first Squadron to be stationed there was No.66 fighter squadron with long range Spitfires. Until this station closed in 1944 many different aircraft were flown from this airfield by many nationalities, but there was always a Spitfire squadron station here. I suppose it was because of the station's remoteness from any big city and night life, it became a posting for the bad lads of Fighter Command."* There were many nationalities including Polish, French, Canadian and Americans as well as British.

The sound of planes landing and taking off was very common and the recently used phrase of, "We counted them out and we counted them back" was a common practice. Arthur Benney recalls seeing our planes leave the aerodrome and often counting a smaller number return. "On the occasions when the entire squadron returned, we didn't have to count; we could read the euphoria in their manoeuvres." Many homes and farms were sacrificed in the creation of the aerodrome and there are many that remember the buildings that now lie below its runways. It still exists as an aerodrome but there is much debate regarding its future.

Part of the Miners Arms was commandeered for military offices during the 2nd World War, it had a close decision between there and Mithian Farm.

I referred earlier to Maggie Dyer from Tuckaway Thatch and Heather Harvey can still remember the wonderful smell as she cooked pasties for the airmen using the ingredients that they had supplied. It sounds as though she was so in demand that she may have been running an early version of the, "Take Away."

The tremendous noise of the American Flying Fortresses hedgehopping as they passed over on their way to France is a memory that has been recalled by many people. Courtney Jenkin said that, "The planes were so low that it seemed as though we could touch them with a long pole."

As in most rural communities, many Mithian families had evacuees living with them and there is mention of this in the Mithian C P School Centenary booklet. Wally Jones and Charlie Newman were both 10-year old evacuees from London. They arrived for a two-year stay in 1940 and lived at Goshen Farm with the Miners family. Ken recalls that the marked contrast with London was difficult for them but that they fitted in very well and attended Mithian School. Charlie had a rude awakening one day when he jumped over a hedge and landed in a wasp nest. He was chased all the way back to the house and, in Ken's words,"He was pickled."

Arthur Benney also recalls the Mithian air raid when a German bomber was chased by Spitfires and jettisoned its bombs down the valley from Lovely Vale. It was reportedly shot down before reaching the coast.

Millicent Rowe managed to cause some panic when she decided to drive the car along Mithian Lane but forgot to use the brake at the junction and shot across the Perranporth to St. Agnes road, hitting the Women's Institute. Jimmy managed to apply the handbrake and reduce the strength of the impact but not enough to avoid the partygoers inside the hall thinking that an enemy bomb had hit the building.

The life of the Land Army girls was far from easy and Avril Chapman recalls having to get up at 5.00am to bring in the cows for milking. Following this, the milk had to be cooled and bottled before being loaded on to the trailer for delivery on the milk round. Returning from the round she could enjoy a one-hour break but then it was time to wash the bottles and prepare for the evening milking session. During the summer, there was the additional work involved in harvesting when full use had to be made of the available daylight hours. The job entailed working a six and a half day week for which she was paid £1 per week with no overtime. Board and lodgings was included with accommodation in the farmhouse. Life was very hard but did have its compensations with frequent social activities being arranged, mostly at the Women's Institute.

Rationing was introduced for the war years and continued after the cessation of hostilities and up to about 1950. The Government issued books of coupons and families used these to obtain their provisions. Many items were in short supply and the system was introduced to ensure that the necessities of life were shared out equally. The following items were affected but the list is by no means comprehensive; flour, butter (2 oz), cheese (4 oz), sugar, bacon (4 oz), tea, fat, margarine, lard, sweets, bread (for a short period) and meat. The system was designed to be fairly rigid but I am told that there was a certain amount of local flexibility!

George Mitchell of Trevellas recalls that in 1940, Mr. Hoare, who lived below Mount May, asked Tom Ford for directions to Wheal Davy Farm where he wanted to visit Henry Johns to buy a harness for his pony. He pointed him in the right direction and told him to take the mine stack as his landmark. With the stack in view he set off on his bicycle travelling past the school and down the hill towards Barkla Shop. On climbing the hill on the road to Wheal Butson he was surprised to find that he had lost his marker. He travelled around for some time trying to catch a glimpse of the mine stack and did, eventually, get to his destination. On his return he asked Tom to point out the landmark again but it was no longer there. At the exact time that Mr. Hoare was in Barkla Shop, and out of view of the stack, the military had blown it up to avoid it being used by enemy planes as a marker for the aerodrome. Wheal Prudence and two other stacks received similar treatment.

During the hardships of the 1930s and the war years, many families turned to keeping chickens and there were some with over a 1,000 birds. George Mitchell recalls that, in the 1930s, timber chicken houses from TLG (Tommy Gill) of Blackwater were 38/- (£1.90) for a 6'x4' shed without a floor or 42/- (£2.10) with a floor.

Mr. and Mrs. Tippett and Ernie and Stanley Chapman collected the old chickens in their pony and trap although what they were used for I am not sure; maybe it was for the zoos.

David Docking was seven when World War II started and he recalls that the children could not appreciate the seriousness of the situation and were very excited by the thought of the fighting. During the early period of the conflict there was a lot of activity when the aerodrome was being built. Lorries carrying hardcore would make their way up from Barkla Shop and boys would suddenly appear and hang off the back of the lorry as it struggled up the hill. He remembers many of the local men going off to war and the influx of RAF personnel and, later, the Americans. He also recalls the Americans having plenty of money that made them very popular with some of the local girls. Apart from the anticipated conflict with the enemy there seemed to be a lot of tension and fights between the white and coloured Americans. David also did a little trading, from a side window of the pub, as he bartered some of his Grandfather's bottles of beer for American gum or whatever.

The children of the village were clearly influenced by the activities of the war when they decided that they would practice parachute jumps off Wheal Liberty viaduct. Maurice Dymond constructed a parachute out of an old blanket, proceeded bravely to his launch point and jumped. He plummeted like a stone and landed in the gorse and bracken. Apparently he was unhurt and a little wiser.

Dandy or dilly racing was very popular with the boys and Henry Solomon remembers spending a lot of time looking for old wheels on the aerodrome. There was always a contest to try and produce a faster machine so that they could become the champion but it seems that no matter what they did, no one could beat Arthur Legg of St. Agnes. Henry's proud boast is that he could free wheel all the way from Goonbell to St. Agnes beach. Apparently it got a bit hairy as you crossed Peterville but there wasn't as much traffic about in the 1940s.

The local ARP group had their Head Quarters at Mithian School and the Mithian Platoon of the Home Guard was in Trevellas Institute. Frank Moore was the Captain of the Home Guard and Hedley Roberts and Leslie Shugg were next in command.

Members of the Home Guard in the photograph from left to right
Back Row - ? Beckett, Fred Brokenshire, Jimmy Green, Jimmy Vincent, Sid Dark, Clem Wills.
Middle Row – Cyril Mannell, Harold Dark, Clifford Mitchell, Jack Holmes (aged 16) Arthur Caunter, Phil Hooper, Henry Ford.
Front Row – Howard Hooper, Les Shugg, Hedley Roberts, Frank Moore, George Symmons.

There were a number of locations used for living accommodation by the RAF and the map shows two of these. Site No. 4 was near the top of Piggy Lane on the left hand side. This was a four-acre field referred to as Mowhay Field. Site No. 5 was located down the lane beside the school and in the field at the rear of Trenoweth, the home of Chris and Maureen Bones.

You will see from the plan that there were numerous buildings on the sites and the following table shows their usage and construction.

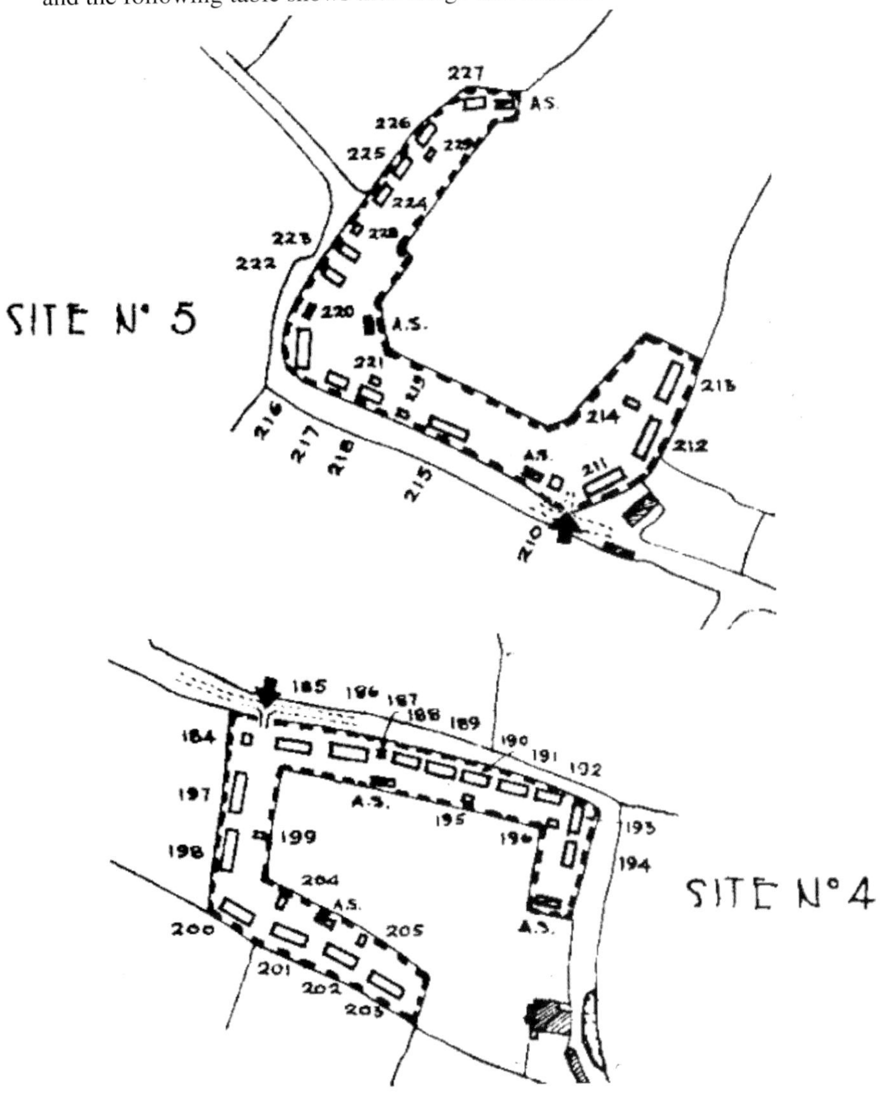

Bldg No.	Building	Type
SITE No. 4		
184	Picket Post	TB
185,186	Sergeants' barrack huts	L
187	Latrines	TB
188,189	Airmen's barrack huts	L
190-194	Airmen's barrack huts	H
195,196	Latrines	TB
197,198	Sergeants' barrack huts	L
199	Latrines	TB
200-203	Airmen's barrack huts	L
204-205	Latrines and drying rooms	TB
SITE No. 5		
210	Picket post	TB
211-213	Airmen's barrack huts	L
214	Latrines and drying rooms	TB
215,216	Airmen's barrack huts	L
217,218	Airmen's barrack huts	H
219,220	Latrines	TB
221	Latrines and drying rooms	TB
222-227	Airmen's barrack huts	H
228	Latrines	TB
229	Latrines and drying room	TB

Buildings: PB – Permanent Brickwork
TB – Temporary Brickwork

Hutting: N – Nissan
L - Laing
H – Handcraft
A – Asbestos
T – Timber
C – Corrugated Iron Sheeting

Shelters: AS – Air Raid Shelter
BS – Blast Shelter
CS – Cycle Stands
GP – Gun Posts

Any information that any ladies can provide about the interior of the buildings will be treated with the utmost confidence!

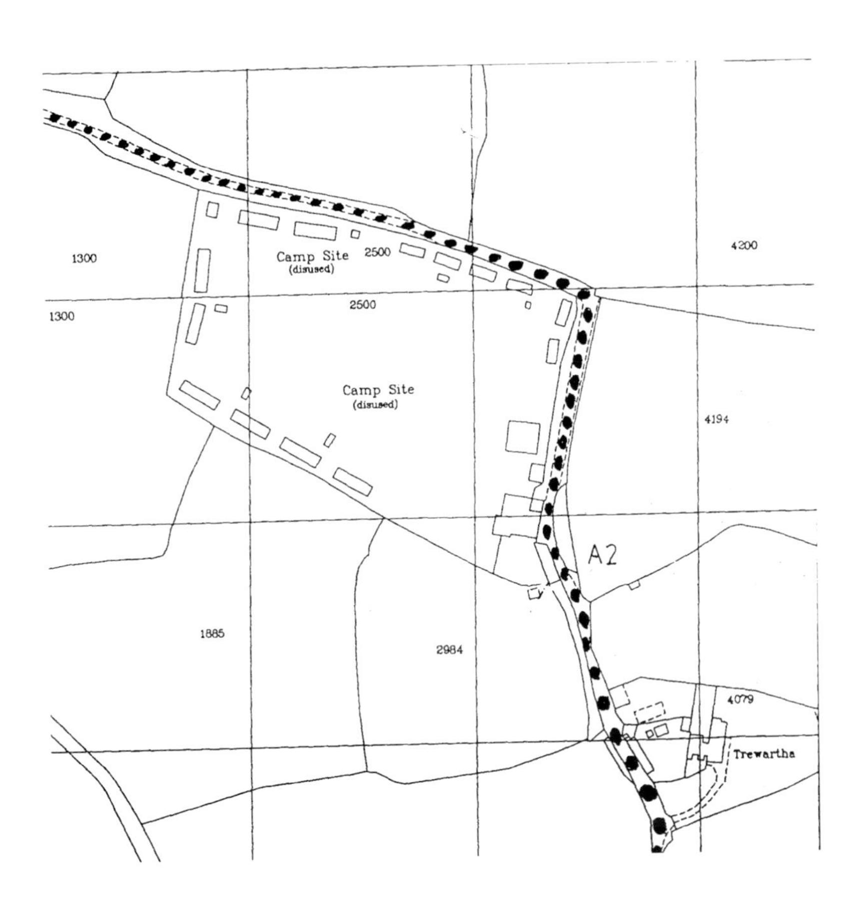

This map is a larger scale and shows the geographical relation of site number 4 and Trewartha Farm

Shops and Businesses

There have been many shops and businesses in and around the village over the years and at one time there were four shops selling groceries at the same time. Whitewalls is now a terrace of three dwellings but at one time it was a row of shops offering clothes, shoes and groceries with the services of the Post Office thrown in.

Mithian Cottage is now a dwelling but as, "The Stores Mithian" it was the last remaining shop in the village until it closed in the early 1990s. Mr. & Mrs. George Rogers (Grandparents to Mrs. Gill-Carey of St. Agnes) ran the shop from the early 1920s to 1932 when Mr. & Mrs. George William Symmons took over. George Henry Symmons, their eldest son, and his wife Muriel succeeded them in 1950 and continued to run it until 1981 when they retired and moved to Perranporth.

George Symmons Jnr. recalls being sent by his father to collect outstanding money and being attacked with a broom by the defaulting customer. It was tough in those days. He also recalls, in the 1950s and early 1960s, collecting the daily papers at Mithian Halt from the 8.00am steam train that had brought them from W H Smith in Truro.

Mr. Symmons provided a delivery service to the more remote parts of the parish. Home and Colonial and the CO-OP also delivered to the village and George Snr. was known to become very annoyed when he saw people who owed him money buying from one of the mobile shops. It was particularly galling when the van stopped outside his premises.

George and Muriel Symmons sold the business to Alan and Sonia (Polly) Fynn who ran it until 1986 when Mr. & Mrs. Roy Siedenburg purchased it and stayed until the early 1990s. It continued as a shop for a few months after they left but Dr. Brian Hope and his wife soon converted it back into a dwelling.

Mrs. Mary Hooper lived in the lower cottage of Whitewalls (now named The Old Post Office) from where she ran a grocer's shop during the late 1890s to about 1915 and her shop sign can be seen in many old photographs of Mithian. Also living there with her were parents, Mr. and Mrs. Whitfield.

Mrs. Edith Mabel Ennor ran a grocer's shop from her home in Ivydene from about 1905 to the 1930s and a photograph of this can be seen earlier in the book. She kept a parrot that shouted, "Shop Mabel!" whenever anyone entered. After Mrs. Ennor's death in 1936 her son, Nicholas Ennor, ran the shop for a short while but he then moved away and the shop closed.

Mrs. Ida Tippett ran a small shop from Manor Cottage during the 1930s. This sold a minimal variety of groceries and could truly be described as a convenience shop.

During the late 1940s and early 1950s, Alwyn (Owen) and Phyllis Russell (daughter of Edward John and Mary Elizabeth Roberts) ran a shop selling bits and pieces at Higher Mithian Farm, Mithian Downs. After it closed they took over a shop at Cameron Estate, St. Agnes.

Mrs. Ellen O'Leary ran the Post Office and a shop in Whitewalls from the very early 1900s to the late 1920s after which, her daughter. Miss Mary Ellen O'Leary took over and continued running it until the early 1950s. At that time the telephone kiosk was located just outside.

On entering the Post Office a bell would ring for what seemed like ages whilst Miss O'Leary made her way from the living quarters. The shop was very dark inside and everything seemed very gloomy. Miss O'Leary was quite short, had her hair tied up in a bun and wore a high boot to accommodate her crippled leg. Her family had originally come from Ireland but in spite of this, she was outwardly very Cornish. She generally agreed with everything that was said indicated either by the short intake of breath through the lips or by exclaiming, "ess", or however it is spelt.

Although Miss O'Leary continued to live in one of the cottages, probably the top one, Mary and Jack Rand took over the Post Office and shop for a few years during the early 1950s.

Mrs. Ivy Elizabeth Proctor then took over as Postmistress and in 1956 transferred the business to Ivydene. It was not long after that the name of the property was changed to Trevene. In 1960 it was transferred back to Whitewalls again when Mrs. Allen became Post Mistress for the next few years.

The Post Office moved to the end of Mithian lane in 1967 when Mrs. Evans took over and ran it for the next 34 years. Her daughter, Janet Evans, succeeded her in 2001 and is the current Post Mistress. Mrs. Evans recalls that there were no responses to the advertisement to run the Post Office and she was approached and asked to take it over. After some consideration and discussion with her husband, she decided to take it on a trial basis. Mr. Evans had to give up his workshop so that it could be converted into the office.

A number of local farmers supplied milk to the village and the outlying houses. Harry Miners (Ken & Roy's father) was farming at Goshen and could be seen with his smart pony and milk float as he made his deliveries. This was in the days before the plastic containers or even the re-usable milk bottles when the milk was dipped out of a churn in a pint or quart measure and poured into the customer's container.

Jack James, who lodged with Miss O'Leary, rented a few fields from Cornwall County Council. He kept a few pigs and also some cows whose milk would be sold to the villagers. The Mitchells at Trewartha Farm had an extensive round which I have mentioned earlier. Jimmy Rowe also supplied milk in the village and with so many providers it makes you wonder whatever did they do with it all?

Greengroceries were supplied from Symmons' shop but a greater selection could be obtained from Arthur Thomas and his horse and wagon or, a little later, from Arthur Benney. I remember Arthur Thomas delivering to Silverwell in the 1950s and the occasion when the horse moved forward pulling the cartwheel over my mother's toe but I can't quite remember what she said. I can also remember that he often called very late in the evening and on one occasion it was past midnight and my father leaned out of the bedroom window and said that we did not want anything that week!

Arthur Benney ran a greengrocery business for about thirty years based at Higher Mithian Farm which covered a large area of St. Agnes parish.

Tonkins of Truro was a supplier of ice prior to refrigerators being in general use. This enabled George Symmons Snr. to introduce the supply of ice cream to the village. The ice was supplied in hessian bags and used to freeze the necessary ingredients. The milk, cream and ice cream powder was poured into a purpose made wooden tub and mixed manually by turning a handle. The finished product was ladled into the wafer maker and sold for 2d each. It was not possible to keep it cold for more than a few hours and George and Ken Symmons remember finishing off the unsold ice cream which had, by then, turned to liquid.

Tonkins of Truro also sold rabbits; part of the rural staple diet. It was certainly a popular item in our family up to the time when the rabbit population was decimated by that evil disease mixamatosis. The dead animals were displayed by having their rear legs linked together and hung on a pole in the back of the van. They also bought rabbits from the locals and George Symmons remembers Tom Dyer and his sons (George and Tom Jnr). and many others catching and supplying these. He also recalls being offered rabbits direct from the catchers in exchange for a packet of Woodbines (cigarettes).

Joe Tamblyn provided a wireless accumulator service, something that was necessary before the coming of mains electricity. A few years later Harry Thomas (son of Elijah Thomas) also provided these. I asked Harry why they were required and he said that it was to charge the valves. That is as technical as this is going to get except that I can remember them as glass containers, about the size of a 2lb bag of sugar, with a handle and filled with acid and plates of metal.

Harry Thomas was born in 1913 and died just prior to this book being finished. At the age of fourteen he started delivering papers for Mr. Richards of St. Agnes. Using his initiative he purchased an engine for charging accumulators which he rented out to his customers. The rental, together with the recharging cost, ranged from 6d to 2/6 for two weeks depending on the size of the accumulator. From this, he moved into selling and repairing radios and, eventually, televisions. His Public Address system was in great demand for all sorts of local events and his was a name that was instantly recognized by most people in the area.

Before the growth of shoe shops in neighbouring towns and before rural folk could afford to buy rather than mend, local cobblers were in great demand and over the years there have been a number of them in Mithian.

George Rogers was a boot maker for many years, probably from 1890 through to 1932. His cobblers shop was located in a timber shed attached to Mithian Cottage and Jack Roberts could recall calling there on his way home from school around 1915 to have a heel or sole re-attached.

According to the 5th edition of Mithian News and Views and referring to cobbler's shops, "......... previous to this it was in a raised wooden building where the telephone is now sited and apparently some boys of the village managed to get a donkey up the steps and into the building without the cobbler knowing. (Whatever are the children of today coming to!!)"

It seems that Mary Hooper's son was a cobbler during the early 1900s and had a shop in the top cottage of Whitewalls. I have not been able to find confirmation of this but if it is true then there would have been two cobblers in the village at the same time.

Another cobbler operating out of a wooden shed was Sid Thomas of Trevellas. His business was located at the end of Mithian Lane and the building was affixed to the end of Corner House. Sid ran the business until his retirement in the 1940s. Fred Docking was also a cobbler around 1939 but although he lived in Mithian, his business was in Mount Hawke and Blackwater.

Up to the time of the birth of shopping centres and the improvement in public transport, Mithian was clearly a self-sufficient village with many essential supplies available within its boundaries. There was even a tailor's shop within the village in 1856 run by Walter Tregelles. I have already mentioned a clothes shop in Whitewalls but it seems probably that Mr. Tregelles was located at Little Willows.

A view of the Post Office and Mrs. Hooper's shop at Whitewalls.

Coal was an essential fuel before the coming of electricity, oil and gas (not that we have the latter yet, of course!) and coal merchants or dealers were very necessary. Mrs. Nicholas Roberts is listed as a Coal Dealer in 1889 and 1893 and Mrs. Annie Roberts in 1897, 1902 and 1906. It seems that the business was simply transferred within the family or that her husband, Nicholas, had died and she started using her own name. Unfortunately I have not been able to determine where they were based.

The Rose family of Montrose started supplying coal around the time of the 1st World War and continued until the sale of the farm in the 1980s. They had an extensive round and there are a number of references to them in this book.

Sidney Shugg (Les Shugg's father) made a living collecting and selling eggs and butter during the 1920s to early 1940s. He carried out his round using a horse and wagon which must have been difficult as he only had one arm. Les Shugg took over from his father and is probably best remembered for selling paraffin from his van.

Just after the 2nd World War many farmers kept poultry and Stanley Ennor, Franklyn Ennor and Les Shugg collected the eggs in their pony and wagons and sold them, mainly in Truro. They shared the facilities of an egg grading, stamping and packing unit located in the lane joining Mithian Downs with Wheal Butson. Jack Roberts had use of this building for a while prior to Higher Mithian Farm being bought by Arthur Benney. It is still in use as a joinery shop and is owned by Andrew Benney (Arthur's son).

There are also a number of businesses that have started in the modern era and who do their bit to put Mithian on the map.

Architectural Design Workshop is based at the Round House and is headed by Barry Ostler. They undertake building design and have carried out many projects both locally and "up country."

Scott and Emma Kemp have operated their Civil Enginering Surveying Company from Trewartha Farm since 1996 carrying out land surveying and associated work.

Derek Gray is a structural engineer and operates from Attwell Farm, Mithian Downs.

Glen-Carne Nurery is situated on Barkla Shop Hill and is run by Mr. and Mrs. Crozier.

ROSE-IN-VALE Country House Hotel and Restaurant is said to have been built as a winter residence by Captain John Oates who was virtually the owner of the Great Wheal Leisure Copper Mine at Perranporth. He was involved in other mines and is said to have controlled all of the mines in the locality. This must have been an elegant private house with its Gatekeeper's cottage at the entrance (on the right as you enter the drive) but it is unlikely that Captain Oates built it. It could be that he refurbished or extended it but he could not have built it. The Tithe map of 1840 shows Capt Oates as the occupier and Sir R. R. Vyvyan as the landowner. I have not been able to determine exactly when Capt Oates took up residence but it was probably during the very early 1800s. He was definitely living there in 1830 up until the 1850s. The weight of evidence suggests that the Nankivells and James lived in the property before Captain Oates and that it was built circa 1770.

The Rev. W. Haslam preached on the lawn of Rose-in-Vale and in his book, "From Death into Life" refers to Capt Oates as, *"....the chief parishioner. He was an uneducated man, who had risen from the rank of a common miner to that of a mine captain."* He further describes him as, *"Being very shrewd and clever and as having succeeded in accumulating a considerable sum of money."* He goes on to say, *"Being the wealthy man of the parish, he sat on Sunday in the large square pew; but beyond giving personal attendance, and that very regularly, I do not know what other heed he gave, either to the service or the sermon."* In another book, Capt Oates is described as, *".... one of the mining kings of the day ...."* Captain William Roberts in his book, "Perranporth", describes him as, *"Uneducated, thrifty, genial, considerate with all ....."* Captain Oates died with no direct relatives and his property passed to Mr. Charles Tregonning. He was buried at Perranzabuloe Parish Church.

Mr. and Mrs. Thomas Nankivell lived here in the late 1700s and John Opie (born 1761), the renowned painter, visited them whilst a young man, his sister being in service there. Ada Earland, in her book JOHN OPIE AND HIS CIRCLE (written in 1911) says, *"Mr. Thomas Nankivell of Rosenvale and his daughter, Joyce, had also been kind to the boy; there is a tradition in the family that Opie painted young Mrs. Joseph Townsend (Joyce Nankivell) out of gratitude for assistance she had given him in his artistic training. Joyce Nankivell was a local beauty, possessing "great sweetness and animation." The name of her father's house, "Rose-in-Vale, is said to have been given as a pretty compliment from a visitor to this fair Cornish flower set in the deep valley in which stood the house."* Joyce has been described elsewhere as, *"The Belle of Mithian."* John Opie lived at Harmony Cott, near Mithian and was indentured to his father who was a carpenter. In this he helped his father with household repairs and was working in Mithian at the house of Benjamin Nankivell when he saw a picture of Ellenglaze farmyard (probably Ellenglaze Manor and farm at Cubert). Lakes, "Parochial History of Cornwall" tells us, *"he would frequently introduce himself on some pretence or other and was observed to take sly peeps upon a farming-picture and then go hastily away to sketch it. He also drew an exact likeness of Mrs. Nankivell's cat."*

According to John Pollock, in his book, "A Very Cornish Practice", it was the home of John James, the founder of Nalders Solicitors, during the early 1780s and through to the turn of the century. He was one of the twenty-four capital burgesses of Truro who were the only people entitled to vote at general elections prior to 1832.

It was sold by auction in 1804 when the estate of John James was wound up (this may well have been the father of the John James referred to above as the lawyer did not die until 1819). The auction notes read, *"Lot 2. For the remainder of 99 years determinable on the death of three lives that* *genteel and modern built dwelling house together with stables, barn, outhouses and about 14 acres. Called Rose-in-Vale, Perranzabuloe occupied by Rev. James Benetto (*possibly Bennets or Benetts*), Clerk, Rent*

£27.2.6 comprising drawing room, dining parlour, hall, kitchen, laundry, dairy, pantry, back kitchen, suitable office, eight bedrooms and being beautifully situated in midst of a fine sporting county, render it a suitable residence for a genteel family."

Also being disposed of by the executors of John James's estate was Wall's tenement occupied by John Oates and Park Hosken house, barn, outbuildings and about 35 acres occupied by John Pearce. (I have been unable to locate Wall's tenement but wonder if it could relate to the walled garden at the rear of Underwood.)

Whilst demolishing a house in Penzance a few years ago some workmen came across a bundle of letters in a cob wall. These were written by a young lady living at Rose-in-Vale and were sent to her fiancée who lived in Penzance. They are dated 1881 and of sufficient local interest to include here. The sending address in each case is Rose-in-Vale St. Agnes, Mithian, Scorrier.

October 26th (18)81

My dearest Herbert

I've just had your letter. Thank you for it my dear. I think Friday will be fine as the barometer is going up. I do hope it will for our first promenade round the garden together – you don't know what pleasure it will be to me, once more to be, walking not hobbling with you again. I shall try to think of the last seven months as only a dream to be forgotten, that is to say, all the pain and trouble, not your care of me, my own, which will never be forgotten. Louisa came down yesterday to induce some of the girls to go to a Missionary Meeting to be held on Friday but they proved "deaf to the voice of the charmer." I have so many pretty things to show you, when you come up, presents most of them –
Yesterday I went into the farm yard and saw the pigs, one of whom is to depart this life next week, having reached such a degree of fat life must be a burden to him. On Monday someone from Scotland came and stopped from 2 o'clock to six, a Mr Sholys (?), I'll tell you all about him, when you come on Friday. I'm going to buy two more pigs. I cannot write more just now darling as I want to take advantage of the noonday sun to get a little fresh air.
Give my love to all at home, especially Harry, whom I hope (or rather we all do) to see soon, and wish very much to yourself my own darling Herby,

I am as ever dearie
Your own Lottie

November 13th (18)81

My dearest Herbert,

I have just read your letter, for which I thank you dear, and am glad you had such nice services yesterday.
With regard to the other matter of which you write, you know I have given you the choice of two things, one of which you must abide by, as I no longer care to lay myself open to unjust suspicions. If you decide that you do not care to come and live here by the time we mentioned, I must then ask you not to come up on Thursday or again, as I am not strong enough to bear an argument on a subject, which can only end one way or the other, though I dare not think what it would be to me if you decide not to come, but

if you think you would not be happy with me, why then my own dear Herbert, I love you too well to wish you to come. As to our being able to get on, miss Lord and myself have told you all we can on the subject. Write soon and tell me your final answer, by return if possible, as the continued anxiety is telling on me very much. I am very grateful to Harry for standing up for me, tell him so please from me.
I cannot write more dear, as I am very tired. I am doing all you told me to do – I shall pray that your decision may be that which will enable me to see you again on Thursday. God help me if it is the other way. Now my dearest <u>my</u> Herbie I must say goodbye,

From your loving Lottie

November 30th (18)81

My own Herbert,

Your letter made me very glad, as it gave me the good news that your cold is better, do my dear be careful, and not get it again. I shall be so glad to see you on Monday week, if you can come away, though I am trying to bear your absence bravely, but it is very hard work, you see you are so thoroughly part of my life, that when you are away I feel all at sea, and hardly able to settle to anything, am I foolish think you?
Oh I nearly forgot to tell you about another present I have had, it is <u>just lovely</u> it is a silver fish slice and fork, one of the handsomest I've ever seen, Mrs William Lord sent it us. I am sure you will like it, everyone thinks it splendid. The servants have given me a cut glass cream glass and jug, very pretty, and Charlie has sent me an Indian white silk shawl to wear on <u>the</u> day. Aunt (Madame Hessen-hut) has sent a pair of vases set in silver, lovely all ferns. Cousin Jim and his wife Hetty have sent a pale blue Indian shawl, and a white Persian one, just grand they are. L and E have ordered a splendid tea and coffee service, and Flo has given us a silver preserve fork, all of these presents have come during the last week, and I expect more yet, shan't we be well off for pretty things? I mean to be <u>quite</u> myself again by the end of the month and will be able to go for a drive with you when next you come, shall you be glad? You do not know how much I look <u>forward</u> to going to Penzance with you. I am always <u>proud</u> to go out with <u>you</u>, and especially in Penzance, what jolly walks we will have again. I think

Richard should play "the Wedding March" at the Recital (I'm only in fun darling). Gracie is staying here for a day or two, as she has been far from well, I am doing all you wish just as if my darling were here, or rather more so, for I obey you much better (for) when you are away than when you are here, as I like to think I am pleasing you. I have worn no long gowns since you have been away, and mean to be very careful when I go for a drive. All send love, and so do I, lots and lots. Now my own darling,

Believe me dearie as ever

Yours Lottie

For those of you who like a happy ending I can tell you that they were married and their wedding is entered in the Parish Register. It was reported in the Royal Cornwall Gazette that a grand wedding took place at Mithian Church on the 10th January 1882 between Miss Charlotte Frewin Lord of Rosinvale and Mr. John Herbert White of Penzance. The bride's father was Charles Frewin Lord (deceased) and her uncle was the Rev. Alfred Lord (deceased) who founded and built St. Peter's Church. The groom, an organist and composer, was the son of Richard White, Professor of Music. Mr. Cooper Furniss of Truro made the wedding cake and Messrs. Henry Andrews and Co of Truro supplied the dresses for the bride and bridesmaids.

John Whitford, a mining captain, lived at Rose-in-Vale from the 1890s until his death in 1926. He was born in 1858 at Newlyn East and moved to Wheal Liberty when he was only a few years old. At the age of ten he walked the five miles to work at West Chiverton mine which took him past Rose-in-Vale which he vowed to buy when he grew up. He spent many years mining in foreign parts before returning to keep his promise. On the 21st February 1881 he married Anne Searle Hooper who was a daughter of Simon Hooper.

Joan Juleff of Bolingey, granddaughter of Capt John Whitford and Anne Searle Whitford, recalls that her mother, Lily Searle Whitford, lived there until 1925 when she married Joseph James Powell Tredinnick who was the son of John Tredinnick of Beacon View, Barkla Shop.

Mr. & Mrs. Reuben Hosken were probably the first to use the property for fee paying guests and ran it as B&B during the 1930s and up to the 2nd World War. Mr. and Mrs. Dores then took it over and ran it as a guest house. They are remembered for keeping geese and growing Pampas grass. This was the era when all rooms were supplied with a jug and bowl for ablutions.

Alan and Jean Turner bought it in 1961 and used it as a base for Piran Pony Stud. During this time some upgrading was carried out including removing the old bedroom fireplaces, and it was awarded a two star rating. Maureen Solomon, who lives at Goshen Cottage, worked for the Turners during their last few years there and continued in 1984 when Vanda and Tony Arthur took over as proprietors.

Vanda recalls that a lot of work has been carried out in re-building, refurbishing and extending the hotel and in 1991 it was awarded a three star rating. Ironically, an old fireplace, probably similar to those removed, has recently been fitted in one of the lounges. The hotel accommodates thirty-four sleeping guests and the restaurant provides for seventy five covers although this increases to 108 in banqueting style. Two rooms were licensed for marriages in June 1995 just two months after the law permitted this.

There are rooms dedicated to Captain Oates and Joyce Nankivel and the dining room is named after John Opie. Copies of John Opie's paintings hang there and the originals are to be found at Trerice Manor and Truro Museum (Royal Institution of Cornwall). In 2003 Vanda and Tony Arthur sold the hotel to Chris and Veronica Thomas and their son Oliver.

The MINERS ARMS (Miners Inn) was a part of Mithian Manor and is undoubtedly a very old building but there are a number of mysteries surrounding it, not least its precise age. Many books state that it was built in 1577; a very precise date that must have been picked up from somewhere. I am not disputing the date but documentary evidence of its age seems nonexistent and I would be interested to know how it was arrived at. It may appear in a history book that I have not read but I have a feeling that it may relate to a date contained in the decorative plaster ceiling of the mezzanine floor. If that is the case then it may well be in error, as reading it in a clockwise direction will reveal that it actually states 1775 and not 1577. There could, of course, be a number of reasons for this. Perhaps an extension was built in 1775 and the original building does date from 1577 – coincidence, but not impossible. Perhaps the ceiling in question was replaced in 1775. Perhaps it is meant to be read anti-clockwise, but why? Or maybe, just maybe, the building is not as old as we had thought.

It has been supposed that the building was used extensively for smuggling and that the tunnel that runs under the road and re-emerges in the Old Manor House was for this purpose. Smuggling was prevalent for a number of centuries but the inn is some way from the coast and the further inland that the merchandise had to be brought the greater the chance of being accosted by the Revenue Men.

It is also suggested that the tunnel could have been a hiding place or escape route for Catholic priests or monks following the Reformation of the mid 1500s and that would make it even older than 1577. This would seem to fit in nicely with the various stories of lost chapels, monasteries and priest holes. This is a period when Cornwall and England were involved in religious persecution of both Catholics and Protestants depending on the persuasion of the particular monarch at the time. During the reigns of Henry VIII and Edward VI Catholicism was heavily suppressed and Mithian Manor was the home of the Wynslades who took part in the Prayer Book Rebellion of 1549 when the Catholic faith and the Cornish language was so resolutely defended.

By the suggested build date of 1577 the Wynslades had long since departed, the Mohuns were in residence and a staunchly Protestant was on the throne once more. It has been rumoured that the clothing and bones of a monk was found in the tunnel but that may just be a bit of garnishing. One final thought on the tunnel and then I will leave it to your imagination. Could it have existed prior to the construction of the building when it would have provided an escape route from the Manor House? Or could it have been a later addition to meet either of the above needs or for a reason not yet put forward? That the tunnel exists is not in doubt; a number of people have looked down into it when it was opened up sometime in the 1960s. Melville Strike says that it was blocked and they did not get very far but that it was clearly the start of a tunnel. Since then, apart from a few bold suggestions at the bar, no further attempt has been made to reopen it.

There are references to Manor Court sessions being held in the building and my feeling is that its history is so linked to the Manor that parts of it must have existed before 1775 and probably before 1577.

I have not been able to find a date when the building first became a tavern but it is included in one listing in 1838. Of course, it may well have operated under another name prior to this and you will read later that there were many other hostelries associated with Mithian.

The Royal Cornwall Gazette of 3rd September 1880 includes a notice, *"TO BE LET and entered upon immediately the MINERS INN situate at MITHIAN in the parish of St. Agnes, together with the grocers & butcher's shop attached and two rich meadows of land. Incoming small. Apply to MOYLE & SON, The Brewery, Chacewater."*

The pub was the subject of a closing order during the late 1800s because it was considered to be a house of ill repute; it had apparently become a base for some ladies-of-the-night.

I have managed to trace the names of tenants or landlords from 1842 but cannot say with any certainty that they are consecutive.

W Mitchell was the tenant in 1842 but he was possibly not the first as it had been a public house or tavern for at least 4 years prior to this.

Wm Letcher took over as landlord in 1856 when the Daveys of Mithian Manor granted him a 99-year lease. In 1873 the property was described as incorporating a grocery and butcher's shop.

H T Bennetts took over in 1879 but it seems that he was found to be drunk on a highway in October of that year and his licence was not renewed. He was declared bankrupt on 24th October 1879, an eventful year for him.

Joseph Sedgman was the landlord in 1889 and 1893.

Charles Tonkin took over in 1896 and, later that year, he was found drunk on leaving his own premises.

Peter Richards was the landlord in 1897 and 1902; a dramatic career change as he had previously been the headmaster of Mithian School. In 1900 and in 1902 he was fined for allowing drunkenness on the premises and in 1903 was found drowned at Perranporth.

In 1905 & 1913 Charles Ellery was in place as landlord.

John Davis was the landlord in 1914 and a report in the Royal Cornwall Gazette on the 4th March 1915 gives an account of a court case involving him.

"At West Powder Sessions on Saturday, John Davis of the Miners Arms Mithian, pleaded guilty to refusing to allow the Police to enter his licensed premises at 11pm on February 13th and also with keeping his house open during prohibited hours. Mr. George S. Bray, (Redruth) appeared for the defendant and pleaded guilty.

P.C.Benney said he went to the house in company with two other constables, and they watched the doors. Witness told the landlord he wanted to inspect the house, but the landlord refused and pushed himself up against the witness saying, "You are not going into my House." Witness moved him out of the way and saw two men named Parsons and Brown, who ran towards the cellars. The men said they had had no drink. Witness pointed out to the landlord that the men had been in the house one hour and five minutes after closing time, and the landlord replied that they had stayed behind to have a chat. The landlord also said the men had not had anything to drink after closing time.

Witness charged him with obstructing him and he replied that he did not want anyone there at that time of night. Witness told him, that according to reports this had carried on for some time.

Mr. Bray: You speak of obstruction, there was no struggle or anything like that?

Witness: No, he put his hand out and simply hindered me for a minute or two.

Mr. Bray said the defendant undoubtedly did a very foolish thing. Mithian was rather a dreary place in the evening and the two men had been there and got into an excited discussion regarding the war. One of them was the landlord's cousin and the landlord gave him a little more latitude than he would have given a stranger. The men stopped in the house but they had no drink. He, Mr. Bray, admitted that the landlord ought to have closed his house but he considered the offence a light one. As to the charge of obstructing the Police there was no intention of being antagonistic to the

Constable, but the landlord evidently wanted to give the men time to escape. There never had been a complaint regarding the conduct of the house, and the landlord had carried on the business to the satisfaction of the Police.

P. C. Benney, recalled, said the two men were quiet and were not drunk.

Defendant was fined £1 and costs for refusing the Constable entrance to his house, and 10 shillings and costs for keeping the house open during prohibited hours.

The two men John Parsons, and William Brown, were each fined 5 shillings and costs for being on licensed premises after permitted hours." (The arresting officer was a great grandfather of Clive Benney who kindly provided this report).

In 1919 John Goodman was the landlord but only for a short period.

James Martin began his lengthy period as landlord in 1919, a stay that was to last for about 30 years. His picture is on the left.
James (Jim) & Gertrude (Gertie) Martin were the parents of Doris who married Fred Docking of St. Agnes

who also lived in the Miners Arms. During the early 1940s, Fred installed electric light to the ground floor of the pub. This was pre-mains electricity and was powered by a generator. This did not extend to the upstairs so it still meant going to bed by the light of a candle. At this time the Landlord's private accommodation was the current lounge bar situated on the left on entering the pub. The kitchen was in its present location but its primary use was for the family as the age of pub food had not yet arrived.

Mrs. Martin had a dislike of women in the bar and did not attempt to disguise her feelings. Her Grandson, David Docking, describes her as having a, "quick" tongue. Life must have been very difficult for her during the 2nd World War when the WAFs from the aerodrome regularly visited the pub.

David recalls that some "black market" pork was hanging in the cellar and mysteriously disappeared at the time when the draymen were delivering. On the next visit she was told that one of the deliverymen was unwell to which she replied, "I expect he's sick of pork." David was born in the Miners Arms and lived there with his parents and sister Jennifer until 1946 when the family moved to St. Agnes.

Jim Martin at the bar when it was located in the window recess

Jim Batten, a relative of Mrs. Martin, also lived there and slept in the small room at the rear of the ground floor dining room. This room, which has been referred to as a Priest's hole or Penance Cupboard, contains the blocked up entrance to the old tunnel that runs under the road to The Old Manor.

Prior to taking the pub, Jim Martin had lived in Mithian for some time and had fought in the Boer War.

Many of the air force men were billeted in Piggy Lane and this proved very convenient for a visit to the pub. Unfortunately the demand often became greater than the supply with the result that the pub ran out of beer. I am not sure if this was due to a general shortage or simply a lack of planning but it must have been equally frustrating for both military and civilian customers.

I have recently seen reference to the 16th century murals and it may disappoint you to learn that these were painted in the 1950s when Bill & Peg Smith were the landlords and it was they who carried out the alterations to the bar area including moving the bar counter from the window recess to its present position.

Desmond (Des) Chapman, shown below, was the landlord from 1958 to 1969, a time when I visited the pub on a number of occasions and can confirm that it was a good house. He was a son of Ernie Chapman and a nephew to Maurice & Jack Chapman.

Les Whear and Jan were here from 1969 to about 1983. He liked brandy and lovage so much that he named his dog Lovage. Les could be very rude to his customers and it was not always easy to tell if he was joking or not. He was proud of anything Cornish and when I once made the mistake of ordering sandwiches before beer he told me, "You're as bad as the b***** English."

Colin Gilham was the landlord from 1983 to 1988, firstly with Sue and, after their separation, with Vicky. During this period the pub developed into a thriving business and it was a good era. They developed the food side and the cellar was opened up and made a very unusual but friendly drinking area. This involved lowering the floor to achieve the required headroom and a local chap, Charlie Williams, undertook the excavation and I imagine that it was tough going in tight conditions. The wall mural in the cellar was painted by Janet Chitty but the area is currently only used for storage.

Peter Andrew was landlord from 1988 to about 1994 when Tony and Pip Richards ran a very busy bar.

Dave & Dyllis Charnock took over in 1994 when a new counter to the public bar was installed.

Richard and Amanda Baylin were in place from 1997 to 2000 before moving to Australia. They introduced the very popular theme evenings with food and wine to match.

Andrew & Michele Bown are the current landlords and have been there since 2000. Andrew is a Cornish "boy" and has previously run other pubs in the locality. The business is currently up for sale and they will be missed.

In 1977 the Devenish Redruth Brewery Ltd purchased the fields at the rear of the pub from Cornwall County Council as part of the disposal of Mithian Farm. This is used as car parking and, by courtesy of the landlord, by the village community for various events. This facility is much appreciated by the villagers as its central position makes it ideal for this purpose.

A building as old as the Miners Arms is certain to have some ghost stories attached to it and there have been a number of unexplained occurrences over the years. Pip and Tony Richards worked here during the late 1980s and there was one bedroom that Pip could not enter due to a, "presence." One of the guests claimed that he received a blow on his back as he descended the stairs. The young children of the previous landlord claimed to have seen a figure. The current landlord, Andrew Bown, has experienced glasses falling off shelves onto the hard floor yet remaining unbroken. On another occasion the sachets of sauces were neatly arranged on the dining room tables at closing time but by the morning had been strewn all over the room. Perhaps a petulant spectre expected more than just the sauces.

My appreciation to John Flanagan who drew this splendid picture of the Miners Arms especially for this book

Mithian was a well-populated mining area with many lead, copper, silver and tin mines and, over the years, there have been a number of Public Houses to serve the villagers. The King's Arms existed in 1811 and at that time the landlady was Jane Coomb and by 1814 someone called Tamblyn had taken it over. In 1841 it was advertised for sale.

The Golden Lion was located in one of the White Walls thatched cottages. The Red Lion and the George III were located at Goshen in Goshen Cottage/Pickety Witch, no doubt to serve the men from the nearby Mine. These may not have been different pubs and may simply have been a change of name. It is, however, probable that there was more than one house in Mithian at the same time but some may have been Kiddly Winks or Penny Houses where a bush would be displayed outside to indicate that a brew was available. One of these is said to have been in Bakery Cottage.

A notice in the newspaper 27th April 1832 reads, *"Unicorn Inn – Mithian St. Agnes. Alice Ennor takes this opportunity of informing her friends and the Public that she has just entered the above named INN and hopes by keeping excellent home brewed beer; spirits of the best quality, well aired beds, good stabling etc, to secure a portion of the public favour, which it shall be her constant study to merit."* In 1836 this public house was taken over by Richard Mitchell.

With so many amenities having been lost to Mithian the Miners Arms has become even more important to the community and it is to be hoped that the interests of anonymous businesses that now seem to control the industry do not affect this.

There have been many businesses based in Mithian and the following pages show commercial undertakings drawn from Trade Directories or other sources. The lists of names and dates show when the businesses were operating. The dates given are those when the survey was carried out so the individuals may have been operating for a few years prior to the first date and for a few years after the second date. For instance, Miss O'Leary followed on immediately after her mother whereas the dates indicate a gap. Where it states, "to after 1939," this is because research has, in most cases, only been carried out to that date.

Amos Gay (farmer) Whitestreet	1856 to 1862
J Woolcock (farmer) Mythian	1856
Wm Letcher, Miners Inn	1873
Theodore Martin (farmer)	1873
Wm Tremewan (shopkeeper)	1873
Wm Henry Hearle, (fmr) Tywarnhayle Fm	1889 to 1897
Dale Martin (fmr) Mithian Farm	1893 to 1902
Misses Mary & Annie Martin (fmr) Mithian Fm	1906
Wm Roberts (farmer) Mithian Downs	1893 to 1910
Vincent Drury-Lowe, Rose-in-Vale	1889
Joseph Sedgman, Miners Inn	1889 to 1893
Mrs Turner, Rose-in-Vale	1893
Charles Doble (shopkeeper)	1889 to 1902
Mrs Nicholas Roberts (coal dealer)	1889 to 1893
Mrs Annie Roberts (coal dealer)	1897 to 1906
Walter Tregelles (tailor) Mythian	1856 to 1889
Samuel Truan (mason)	1889
Thomas Truan (mason)	1889
Alfred Martyn, Rose-in-Vale	1897
William Henry Bartle (carrier)	1889 to 1906
William Henry Bartle (farmer)	1910
John Henry Bartle (fmr) H. Penwartha	1897
James Cocking (fmr) Mithian Downs	1893
Mrs Jane Cocking (farmer) Mithian Downs	1897 to 1910
R Crebo (blacksmith) Mythian	1856
Alfred Crebo (blacksmith)	1889 to 1906
Mrs Frances Mary Hooper (shopkeeper)	1897 to 1914
Mrs Richard May (farmer)	1897

Mr. Richards (Board Headmaster) Bucks Head	1878
Joseph Vivian (paint manufacturer) Barkla Shop	1878
John Henry White (farmer) Rose-in-Vale	1883
Peter Richards, Miners Inn	1897 to 1902
George Rogers (boot maker)	1893 to 1919
George Rogers (shopkeeper)	1923
Mrs P Rogers (shopkeeper)	1926 to 1930
John Rose (farmer)	1889 to after 1939
Edward John Roberts (fmr) Mithian Downs	1914 to after 1939
James Tredinnick (farmer)	1897 to 1906
Joseph Brown (farmer)	1902
Charles Ellery, Miners Inn	1906 to 1910
Mrs Mabel Edith Ennor (grocer)	1906 to 1930
Nicholas Ennor (grocer)	1935
Henry Thomas Harris (carpenter)	1906
Mrs Ellen O'Leary (sub-postmistress)	1906 to 1926
Miss Mary Ellen O'Leary (sub-postmistress)	1930 to after 1939
John E Tremewan (shoolmaster)	1906
Morley B Collins	1910
John Tredinnick (bldr) Beacon View	1910 to 1919
Samuel Woolcock (fmr) Trewartha Fm	1910 to 1919
James Woolcock (fmr) Trewartha Farm	1923 to 1930
Thomas Henry Bartle (butcher)	1914 to 1930
John Davis, Miners Inn	1914
Arthur Goyne (fmr) Mithian Downs	1914
Henry Stephens (farmer) Wh. Davy	1914 to 1926
James Thomas Tamblyn (farmer)	1914 to 1930
Misses Lydia & Mary Tresize (fmr)	1914 to 1919
Thomas Wellington (fmr) Mithian Dns	1914 to 1923
John Goodman, Miners Inn	1919 to 1923
James Henry Martin, Miners Inn	1930 to after 1939
Rev John Jones, Vicarage	1923
Capt Joseph James Hooper (farmer)	1923 to 1926
Henry Johns (farmer) Goshen	1923 to 1926
Henry Johns (farmer) Wh Davy	1930 to 1955
Charles Roberts (farmer) White St	1923 to 1935
Rev Phelps, Vicarage	1930 to 1935
John Bartle Whitestreet	1930 to 1935
Frederick Biscombe (fmr) Mithian Dns	1930
Reuben Hoskin, Rose-in-Vale	1930 to after 1939
Stanley Williams (farmer)	1930 to after 1939
Rev Philip Latham, Vicarage	1935 to after 1939
Charles Brokenshire (farmer)	1935 to after 1939

Thomas John Glasson (farmer)	1935 to after 1939
John Mitchell (farmer) Trewartha	1935 to after 1939
George Wm Symmons (shopkeeper)	1935 to after 1950
George Henry Symmons	1950 to 1986
Wm Jn Chhristopher (fmr) Whitestreet	1939 to after 1939
Johnson Jason Moyle (farmer) Mithian Downs	1930 to after 1939

Transportation

Up to the early 1800s most people travelled on foot or, if you were more fortunate, by horse. This had been the mode of transport for generations and the roads were little more than tracks that had been shaped by regular usage.

These tracks were used by mules carrying minerals from the mines to the ports, by cattle travelling from field to farm and by villagers for their daily travel. During winter months these tracks must have become mud baths. These familiar routes were probably used in our current road layout but there would also have been other lanes such as through Mithian woods and along the water leat to Magor's Mill. The road that now leads to Mithian Downs is relatively new and discussions were under way in 1847 to extend this to meet the St. Agnes to Truro turnpike road. This was clearly not the main southern exit from Mithian in the early 1800s.

A bus service through the village was provided by Elijah (Liech) Henry Thomas and during the 1930s to the early 1940s he ran 10.00am and 2.00pm services on Wednesdays and Saturdays to Truro and on Fridays to Redruth. Elijah lived in Trevellas and had two children; Lillian, Queenie (wife of the late Roy Miners) and Harry Thomas.

Elijah started his bus service before the 1st World War with a second hand, purpose built bus pulled by a single horse. He had purchased it from John Mitchell whose father, Harry Mitchell, had run a service from

about 1900 to his death in 1907. Over the years the bus deteriorated and was replaced with a new one built by Frank Piper of Trevellas but this was a much more basic vehicle. During the late 1920s he decided to dispense with traditional horse power and he bought a motor bus which was a second hand Italia Frashina named, "The Lion" which had seen service as a lorry during the 1st World War. Ward's Garage at Chiverton Cross built a coach body for it and Elijah had the first in his line of mechanised transport. Running on its solid tyres it was used for the regular service runs and for Bank Holiday trips to the beach. Elijah's son, Harry, revealed one drawback with the vehicle. The brakes were connected to the transmission belt so if that broke then both drive and brakes were lost. On the basis of, "if something can go wrong then it will", the worst happened by the Railway Station in Truro and the bus careered down over Richmond Hill eventually slowing on the cobbled surface in Ferris Town and Frances Street. A short walk up the hill to collect the broken belt was followed by a rejoining operation and they were on their way once more. After about five years, "The Lion" suffered an ignominious end when it was converted to a chicken's house. It was replaced by a large Humber car and then by a Fiat, 14 seater, soft-top "Bluebird," a name that was to be used for the "fleet" from then on. A Chevrolet 14 seater followed and a Bedford eventually replaced this.

The police were very strict about overloading and standing passengers were not allowed. Anyone without a seat was told by the driver to either walk down the hill from Highertown or "clucky" down whilst in the city area. Just to keep in with the constabulary one of the policemen was regularly given a free ride to the police station – standing of course. During this time a taxi service was also provided with the vehicle driven by Harry.

Elijah died on the 14th February 1954 and his wife continued to run the business for a short time with the help of Harper and Kellow and a borrowed driver but the business was eventually sold to Mr. Walker who ran it during the 1950s. Harper & Kellow eventually took over the route and the business was eventually sold to C R Williams and then to Truronian.

The railway from Chacewater to Newquay was constructed by Arthur Carkeek of Redruth in accordance with the Great Western Railway Act of 1897. It provided a valuable service from 1903 to 1963 and there were many who came to rely on it and mourned its demise. Like many other branch lines that disappeared under Dr. Beeching it is remembered with considerable nostalgia. An entry in Kelly's Directory in the early 1900s reads; *"The Gt. Western Railway motor car service from Chacewater to Newquay has a "Halt" at Mithian."* The Halt itself opened in August 1905, a couple of years after the line was brought into use.

It is recorded that the railway opened to the sound of detonators at St. Agnes and Perranporth stations and that the railway buildings were gaily decorated with bunting.

A great number of people came to Cornwall to help with the building of the railway including Bill Brown and his brother-in-Law, Fred White. The route included many hills and valleys and it must have come as quite a relief to the navvies when they came across a length of level ground.

M. H. Bizley, in his book, "Friendly Retreat" schedules the minimum heights and spans of the individual arches and bridges, together with the

TRURO, CHACEWATER, PERRANPORTH AND NEWQUAY (One class only).

		WEEK DAYS.												SUNDAYS Commences May 16th 1937.			
		a.m.	a.m.	a.m.	a.m.	a.m.		p.m.	p.m.	p.m.	p.m.		p.m.	a.m.	p.m.	p.m.	p.m.
TRURO	dep.	5 55	....	7 35	9*50	11 25	Saturdays only until May 29th, 1937. Each week-day commencing May 31st.	12 35	3 20	4 35	6 0	....	8*30	9 15	12 30	2 40	6 5
CHACEWATER	dep.	6 5	6 42	7 46	10 7	11 37		12 46	3 31	4 46	6 11	..	8 43	9 26	12 41	2 51	6 17
Mount Hawke Halt	"	May 15th and Sats. commencing June 5th, 1937	6 47	7 51	10 12	11 42		12 51	3 36	4 51	6 16	....	8 48	9 31	12 46	2 56	6 22
St. Agnes	"		6 52	7 56	10 17	11 47		12 56	3 41	4 56	6 21	..	8 53	9 36	12 51	3 1	6 27
Goonbell Halt	"		6 55	7 59	10 20	11 50		12 59	3 44	4 59	6 24	....	8 56	9 39	12 54	3 4	6 30
Mithian Halt	"		7 0	8 4	10 25	11 55		1 4	3 49	5 4	6 29	..	9 1	9 44	12 59	3 9	6 35
Perranporth Beach Halt	"		7 5	8 9	10 30	12 0		1 9	3 54	5 9	6 34	....	9 6	9 [illegible]	1 4	3 14	6 40
PERRANPORTH	"		7 8	8 12	10 33	12 3		1 12	3 57	5 13	6 37	..	9 10	9 52	1 7	3 17	6 43
Goonhavern Halt	"		7 16	8 20	10 41	12 11		1 20	4 5	5 21	6 45	....	9 18	10 0	1 15	3 25	6 51
Shepherds	"		7 23	8 27	10 48	12 18		1 27	4 12	5 28	6 52	..	9 25	10 7	1 22	3 32	6 58
Mitchell & Newlyn Halt	"		7 26	8 30	10 51	12 21		1 30	4 15	5 31	6 55	....	9 28	10 10	1 25	3 35	7 1
Trewerry & Trerice Halt	"		7 31	8 35	10 56	12 26		1 35	4 20	5 36	7 0	..	9 33	10 15	1 30	3 40	7 6
NEWQUAY	arr.		7 38	8 42	11 3	12 33		1 42	4 30	5 43	7 7	....	9 40	10 22	1 37	3 47	7 13

		WEEK DAYS.									SUNDAYS Commences May 16th, 1937.			
		a.m.	a.m.	a.m.	p.m.		p.m.	p.m.	p.m.	p.m.	a.m.	p.m.	p.m.	p.m.
NEWQUAY	dep	7 43	8 50	11 30	12 40	Saturdays only until May 29th, 1937, Each Week day commencing May 31st.	1 47	4 43	6 5	7 20	10 30	1 45	4 40	7 25
Trewerry & Trerice Halt	"	7 50	8 57	11 37	12 47		1 54	4 51	6 12	7 27	10 37	1 52	4 47	7 32
Mitchell & Newlyn Halt	"	7 56	9 3	11 43	12 53		2 0	4 57	6 18	7 33	10 43	1 58	4 53	7 38
Shepherds	"	8 1	9 8	11 48	12 58		2 5	5 2	6 23	7 38	10 48	2 3	4 58	7 43
Goonhavern Halt	"	8 6	9 13	11 53	1 3		2 10	5 7	6 28	7 43	10 53	2 8	5 3	7 48
PERRANPORTH	"	8 14	9 20	12 2	1 11		2 17	5 14	6 36	7 50	11 0	2 15	5 10	7 55
Perranporth Beach Halt	"	8 15	9 21	12 3	1 12		2 18	5 15	6 37	7 51	11 1	2 16	5 11	7 56
Mithian Halt	"	8 22	9 28	12 10	1 19		2 25	5 22	6 44	7 58	11 8	2 23	5 18	8 3
Goonbell Halt	"	8 28	9 34	12 16	1 25		2 31	5 28	6 50	8 4	11 14	2 [illegible]	5 24	8 9
St. Agnes	"	8 31	9 37	12 19	1 28		2 34	5 31	6 53	8 7	11 17	2 32	5 27	8 12
Mount Hawke Halt	"	8 35	9 41	12 23	1 32		2 38	5 35	6 57	8 11	11 21	2 36	5 31	8 16
CHACEWATER	arr	8 40	9 46	12 28	1 37		2 43	5 40	7 2	8 16	11 26	2 41	[illegible] 36	8 21
TRURO	arr	8 50	10*0	12 37	1 47		2 53	6* 0	7 12	8*28	11 36	2 51	5 [illegible]	8 31

width of roadway, which was necessary to carry the railway. For instance, most of the bridges over the narrow roads were 14 ft. height and 12 ft. span whilst the roadway over the railway from St. Day, Whitestreet to Mithian Village was to be 15ft wide. The St. Day mentioned here relates to Silverwell Farm which is just beyond Mithian Downs when travelling from the village.

The viaduct between Goonbell Halt and Mithian is a fine example of railway construction and is also aesthetically very pleasing. Constructed out of local stone, it was the last to be built in Cornwall. Its use was discontinued when the line closed under the Beeching era but it still stands and looks as impressive as ever.

The branch line from St. Agnes to Perranporth opened on the 6th July 1903 and pupils from Mithian School were given a free ride to Perranporth and back.

The journey from Perranporth to Mithian was a tough uphill climb where the train slowed to crawling pace. It is very evocative to recall the sight of smoke rising from the fields as the steam train made its way through one of the many cuttings on its journey from Mithian Halt back to Chacewater via Goonbell Halt, St. Agnes Station, Mount Hawke Halt and over the old A30 road at Blackwater. I can recall using these points of departure on lengthy journeys to watch local football (soccer) matches. This 1905 photograph shows the steam unit on its journey to Perranporth.

Arthur Benney remembers the island platform being built at St. Agnes station in 1937, this provided a passing place for the single track and was necessary because of the delays being experienced whilst waiting for trains to reach one end or the other. The construction of the platform and passing place involved the combined labours of 50 to 60 local men and must have been very welcome at a time when work was not all that plentiful. Arthur can also remember the last load of cattle travelling on the line when the Bradley family moved from Wheal Butson back to Wales.

Ken Miners recalls using the line daily on his journey to school in Truro via Chacewater during 1939 to 1944. The cost of the trip was seven pence (approximately three new pence) per day return. Heather Harvey remembers the delays at Chacewater station during the war when priority had to be given to the troop trains. This could be up to an hour and there was always a couple of extra sandwiches in the lunch box just in case. She also remembers walking home from Mithian Halt after school with Dawn Shugg and combining this with bringing the cows in for milking.

During the 2nd World War many servicemen were billeted at the top of Piggy Lane (and elsewhere) and it became a familiar sight to see them walking up through the village from the train to their temporary home.

John Flanagan recalls travelling the line in the late 1940s and early 1950s. One of the guards always wore a rose in his lapel and would ask John to turn out the lamp as he left the Halt.

During the late 1950s to its closure in 1963, John Eley worked as a maintenance man on the Goonhavern to Blackwater bridge section of the line. He remembers having to attend a medical at Plymouth prior to be taken on. This involved looking through a pair of very old and battered spectacles and being asked if he could see anything. He replied, "Not a thing" and was told, "You'll do." His medical was completed so quickly that his wife, Margaret, had not even entered the first shop on her shopping spree.

There were five men working on his stretch of track and a further four to cover Goonhavern to Newquay. During the summer months they were busy trimming the banks and hedges bordering the track and he recalls that there were often fires caused by the sparks and clinker being blown out by the steam engines, particularly the older models. This often set fire to the fencing and the fields of corn alongside the track. In this event, compensation had to be paid to the farmers. It was also necessary to maintain the track and the five men would work on this for about four months a year. This involved loosening the chair bolts, unbolting and oiling the chairs, winding down the bolts and tightening them. It was also necessary to oil the slotted fishplates at the junctions of the tracks lengths and he painfully remembers this as being a favourite place for nesting wasps.

During periods of wet weather the men sheltered in huts made out of sleepers. Firemen on passing trains occasionally threw off coal so that they could build a fire in the hut for heat or to warm their pasties. Their transportation consisted of a motorised trolley that ran along the railway track. This was a one-ton capacity vehicle powered by a Ford V8 engine and was designed to carry six to eight people. There was, of course, no need for a steering wheel but it had a number of gears that were used in either forward or reverse mode. It carried its own derailing equipment to enable it to be removed from the track very quickly although there was a very efficient alerting procedure that ensured that they would not be mown down by the next train bound for Newquay. There was also a small two-man version available to them and this could be lifted on and off the tracks by its wooden handles.

John explained that one rail was always higher than its partner, even on flat stretches. This may only be by half an inch but was sufficient to keep the bogey wheels running true. On corners there may be a difference of four inches and with the arrival of the longer diesel units a lot of damage was caused to the rails as they negotiated the relatively tight bends.

During the winter months it was necessary to check and build up any lengths that had dropped in level. Siting boards were used to check the height and the ballast had to be moved to enable the sleepers to be packed up. The ballast was shovelled back onto the sess (a footpath made from ashes) and chippings barrowed from the stockpiles along the edge of the track. A special cup was used to measure the quantity of chippings required as determined by the siting process. The chippings were spread under the raised sleeper and the next passing train would compress it. As John says, "It was just like rolling pastry." John enjoyed his time on the railway and regrets its passing.

There was one level crossing in the area but it was not located on a public road. In 1961 an agreement was drawn up between Cornwall County Council and the British Transport Commission to close the crossing located on Mithian Farm land just below the present golf range.

Sadly the railway line from Chacewater to Newquay closed in 1963 and the picture shows the track being removed.

During the 1800s the upkeep of the roads was undertaken by The Board of Highways and the following extracts relate to the Mithian area.

24th February 1842 - "Resolved that the hedge of James Martin's field be built to a proper height"
"That the surveyor be allowed to offer as much as 7/6 per yard for what load may be required to widen the road from Barkla Shop to Mithian."

26th May 1842 - "Resolved that in widening the Road from Barkla Shop to Mithian that the Surveyor be authorised to raise about 300 load of stone and that the same may be sold to Mr. John Woolcock at sixpence per load of 20 cwts."
"Resolved that two men be employed to remove the earth from Mr. Woolcock's Mowhay to raise the road through Mithian Town." This, undoubtedly, refers to the road in front of the Manor complex at the bottom of Chapel Hill.

29th December 1842 – "Resolved that the surveyor do repair the road leading from Barkla Shop to Mithian Downs. Resolved that Mr. Newton not having accepted the offer made him by the Board respecting the taking down of Simon Tonkin's House, that Messrs Letcher Chellew, Williams & Nettle do call on Mr. Abraham Mitchell and arrange with him for a part of his orchard and garden subject to the confirmation of the Board."

30th May 1844 – "The committee appointed to inspect and report the present state of the road at Barkla Shop reported as follows. That the Bridge be lengthened southward as far as may be found necessary that the road be widened through Barkla's Garden and also from the entrance to Teague's House to the road leading to Mithian Downs."
"Resolved that the above report be carried into effect forthwith under the direction of the following cmttee:- - "
"Resolved that John Gill be advanced in his wages 2/- week for 20 weeks which money is to be laid out by the surveyor in clothes for him."

29th August 1844 – "Resolved that the surveyor sell all stone raised in improving the road near Barkla Shop which will not be required for the use of the Parish at the rate of 10d per load."
"Orders that the surveyor call all the members of the Board to meet at Barkla Shop to look at the state of the road at the top of the Hill Bucks Head and on the top of the hill at Vellanoweth with the view of improving the road at the said hills."

12th September 1844 – "The Board having met at Barkla Shop according to notice. Resolved that the top of the hill at Bucks Head be cut down so as to make a gradual rise from Crebos Shop up to John Williams house and that the road be widened at the west side thereof in Firstbrook's field – also that the top of the hill be taken down to the west of Barkla Shop Bridge the north hedges from the quarry to the gate at Vellanoweth. I sign for the west hill. John Woolcock."

24th April 1845 – "It was proposed and carried that the following persons form a committee to view and report to the Board their opinion as to the best course to be taken to improve Bucks Head Hill and that the Committee goes on the spot the last Thursday in May at 3 o'clock for that purpose and that / form a Koram. (11 names)"

29th May 1845 – "Carried that the repairs of Bucks Head Hill be postponed for 12 months" .

7th January 1847 – "The surveyor having reported that Mr. Woolcock is about to take down his old Smith's shop at Barkla Shop and that he is about to build a new one and as a piece of ground there may in time be of service to widen the road. Resolved that the surveyor call a meeting of the whole Board on an early day to go on the spot and determine whether it is desirable to purchase and if so to complete a purchase."

20th May 1847 – "An application was made by letter from Mr. Richard Davey requesting that the road be repaired leading from Mithian over Mithian Downs to Blackwater. Deferred till next meeting."
"Moved by Mr. Lawry and seconded by Mr. Newton that a Committee be appointed to inspect Barkla Shop Hill and direct the cutting down of the same and that the following form the committee (6 names). Resolved that one hundred pounds be borrowed to pay the men employed instead of making a rate – the money to be borrowed on the best terms."

2nd September 1847 – "Application was made by Mr. Davey for the continuance of the road leading from Mithian village to the Turnpike Road that leads to the Chiverton Arms – agreed to."
"Resolved that William Cockin, in future be paid one shilling and two pence per diem. Thomas & Peter Harris to be no longer employed – Joseph Tonkin to receive one week's notice to be dismissed. John Will's boys to receive the same. John Harris's boys and Anne Martin to be no longer employed on the roads."

George Symmons recalls that the roads were repaired on the basis of the council providing the material and hiring in gangs to lay it. The men would live in the covered trailers that were pulled by the steam engines. On one such occasion, just after the war, the roads around Mithian were due for repair and the road workers moved into the village. During the week that they were here they ran up a bill of about thirty shillings (£1.50 but quite a lot of money in those days) in Mr. Symmons shop and left before paying. George is still waiting for settlement!

People

This is a very difficult section as there are so many people that live, or have lived, in Mithian that deserve a mention. In a book of this size it is not possible to name them all and I hope that my selection will not cause too much disappointment.

The census is a very helpful research instrument and there are some interesting facts and conclusions that can be drawn from it.

In 1841 the predominant occupations for men, and some women, was (i) miner, either tin, copper or lead and (ii) farmer. In the case of mining, sons would follow fathers underground as in the case of John Thomas and his son, John and Joseph Cook and his son Henry. There were, of course, a number of other related and non-related occupations undertaken by the people of Mithian and the following are just a sampling.
Martha Boundy aged 15 was a tin dresser.
Jane Roberts aged 15 was a field breeder.
Elizabeth Boundy aged 50 was a wash woman.
Mary Roberts aged 50 was a charwoman.
John Woolcock aged 40 was a farmer.
James Ennor aged 25 was a miller.
James Ennor aged 60 was a yeoman.
Joseph Tregelles aged 50 was a shoemaker.
William Delbridge aged 60 was a stonemason.
Elizabeth Menadue aged 20 was a tailoress.
William and Mary Michell both aged 30 were innkeepers with six children aged four months to 16 years old.
John Pearce aged 15 was a clock and watch apprentice.
William Tremewan aged 40 was a blacksmith.
There are also milliners, sawyers, carpenters and a few lucky people of independent means.
John and Joan Oates were living at Rose-in Vale at this time.

Common names of this time are Delbridge, Roberts, Chynoweth, Barkle, Woolcock, Thomas, Ennor, Blight, Nankivel, Harris, Jenkins, Hooper, Whitford and Mitchell (various spelling).

The majority of families had six or more children, many reaching this size whilst the wife was still in her twenties. Whilst some people lived to a good age there are many instances of widows or widowers being left to raise a large family. There was a young family called Cook where Nicholas aged

25 was a tin miner, his wife Harriet aged 15 and their daughter, Elizabeth aged eight months. At this time people did not move far from their roots and in almost every case the birth is shown as Cornwall.

As we move to the census of 1851 there are some additional interesting points.
A number of men and women, mostly elderly, are recorded as being supported by Parish relief and a number of properties are shown as being uninhabited.
Nicholas and Harriet Cook have remained together and now have five children including John aged eight who is working as a farmer's boy.
Thomas James aged 66 is a schoolmaster (almost certainly at a private school as state education had not yet started).
Walter Tregelles aged 31 is a master tailor employing two hands.
Richard Michell aged six is an errand boy.
Thirze Woolcock aged 48 is a farmer with 150 acres and employing six labourers. He is a widower with three sons and four daughters. One of the sons, William Woolcock, is a blacksmith.
James Ennor aged 30 is a traveller in hardware.
Capt John Oates is still living at Rose-in-Vale but he is now 82 years old and has been widowed. His niece, Betty Lowry, lives with him together with three servants, James James (coachman), Susan James and Sally Nicholls.
Amongst other occupations there are malsters, copper ore dressers and waggoners and the surname of Shugg appears.

In 1871 we find the Cook family but this time it is Nicholas aged 24, his wife Mary and their son John Henry aged three who is described as a scholar.
James Nile aged 26 and his wife, Jessie aged 23, are farmers at Harmony Cott with 10 acres.
Elizabeth Gatley aged 59 is a farmer's widow.
Sarah Nile aged 55 is a carpenter's widow.
William Letcher aged 53 is an innkeeper with his wife, Susan Ann, aged 49.
Daughters Dorothy aged 19 is a barkeeper and Christian aged 15, is a scholar.
Theodore Martin aged 42 is a farmer with 200 acres with a wife Elizabeth aged 33. They have a daughter Annie aged four and two sons; James aged six and Stephen Dale aged one. No doubt the same Dale Martin who appears later as farming at Mithian Farm. Jane Pearce also lives with them as their servant.
Walter Tregelles, tailor, still appears with his wife Jane aged 47.
Elisha Berryman aged 61 is a mine clerk and has a wife, Mary who is 52.

William Tremewan aged 73 is a grocer and a widower.
Fanny Hooper aged 36 is a lead miner's widow with seven children aged between three and 16.
Harriet Ashman aged 29 is a widow with two children and is described as a Marino store collector.
Richard Hawke is a licensed hawker.
John Whittle aged 52 is a boot and shoemaker and has a wife Ann aged 50.
Margaret Hooper aged 71 is a schoolteacher.
Simon Hooper aged 39 is a lead miner and he and his wife, Sarah aged 36, have four children, Ann Searle, Lydia, Simon and Albert Edward.
Martin Ennor aged 40 and his wife, Louisa aged 38, have five children including Nicholas aged nine months and Frank aged two years.
Richard Cowling has been living and farming Rose-in-Vale since the 1850s. He is described as a farmer with 80 acres employing two men and two boys. His wife is called Annie and they have two servants.
One person, who I have chosen not to name, is categorised as an idiot.

It is noticeable that in many cases, different generations lived in the same house indicating the tendency for families to, "take care of their own."

In 1891 Rose-in-Vale is occupied by widower Joanna Jennings aged 82. Her daughter, Mary A Tucker and grandson Wm Tucker, live with her.
Catherine Bennetts aged 76 and a widower lives in Rose-in-Vale Cottage and is described as an annuitant. Her unmarried son, Thomas Bennetts and her married daughter, Ann Mitchell, live with her.

In 1891 we find that Simon Hooper aged 59 is now a widower living with his daughter, Lydia, aged 23.
James Ennor aged 76 and his wife, Maria aged 68, are dairy and poultry keepers.
Peter Richards aged 58 is the schoolmaster at the State school. He was the Head Teacher from the school's opening in 1874 until 1896 after which he became landlord at the Miners Inn.
George Rogers aged 26 is a shoemaker and is married to Phillippa aged 22.
Mary A James aged 62 is a farm labourer.
Thomas Cowling aged 36 is a grocer.
Norman Turner aged 33 and his wife, Jessie, aged 27 are living in Rose-in-Vale and are described as, "living on own means." They have a son of ten months and employ two servants who are single girls from London.

At the turn of the century, in 1901 there is an increase in the number of people, "living on their own means." The occupation of tin miner still appears but is less common. There are many householders with boarders

and this may have been due to the construction of the new railway that ran through Mithian and on to Perranporth. One thing that still applies is the vast majority of entries being of Cornish birth. The names are now beginning to become more familiar and many appear elsewhere in this book.
Reuben James aged 28 and his wife, Lydia, have one daughter at this time, Lydia Pearl aged one.
Mary Doble aged 39 is a shopkeeper.
Mary Hooper aged 33 is also a shopkeeper and was born in Plymouth. Living with her is her father and mother, Wm and Elizabeth Whitfield aged 74 and 65. She also has a boarder, John Quick aged 33.
Mrs. Ellen O'Leary aged 39 lives with her daughter, Mary aged nine and her son, Jeremiah aged eight. She also has two boarders; Thomas Claude aged 60 is a foreman on the railway works and Edward Rowe aged 60 is a labourer.
George Rogers is now aged 35 and is a boot and shoemaker. His wife, Phillipa, is aged 32 and shown as coming from St. Agnes.
James and Annie Tamblyn are aged 22 and 24 respectively.
Peter Richards aged 67 is the landlord at the Miners Inn with his wife aged 42 and six children. Also living with them is Mary Ann Crebo aged 85, his mother-in-Law.
Stephen Dale Martin aged 31 is a farmer living with his two sisters; Annie aged 34 and Mary aged 24. They have a live-in servant, Ellen Mannell.
Sam Woolcock aged 47 lives at Trewartha Farm with his wife, two daughters and son, James.
Mary Hooper aged 26 is a married lady from Ireland and lives with her children Tammy aged three, who was born in South Africa, James aged two and Gwendoline aged one.
John Magoe aged 44 is a farmer living with his wife, Sarah, aged 40, John aged six and Llewellyn aged two.
The Whitford family are living in Rose-in-Vale although the head of the house, Capt John Whitford, is absent and probably mining in South Africa. His wife, Ann Searle Whitford is aged 41 and living with her three sons and two daughters. Three of her children were born in Johannesburg.
Frank and Annie Ennor appear with their three infant sons, Franklin, John and Raymond.
William and Alma, Fanny Rose are in their 40s and have three children, John, Mabel and Hetty.
Thomas Henry Bennetts is now aged 56 and living with his wife, Betsy, aged 45 at Rose-in-Vale Cottage.
Names like Brokenshires, Harvey, Dobles, Evans and Brewers begin to appear.

Kernick Eley was born at Penhallow in 1911 and died in 1995. He married Marjorie Angove in 1937 in Penzance and their daughter, Joan, was born the following year. They lived in Newlyn at this time, in No 1 Farmer's Meadow.

In 1951 they moved to Goverley, Mithian Downs and lived in a caravan until they had finished converting the barn into a dwelling.

Marjorie's parents had lived in a cottage nearby but, following Mrs. Angove's death in 1950, this was abandoned but the ruins can still be seen.

Like a number of women in the area, Marjorie worked in the Newquay Knitting Mills, travelling each day by train from Mithian Halt. Kernick worked for James George Brewer of Perranporth and Joan can recall him having to travel to Falmouth on a shared bicycle. The first rider would set off for a mile or so and then leave the bike in the hedge for the second person, who was walking, to reach there and have his turn to ride. He would cycle past his mate who would then pick up the bike in due course. All this before carrying out a full days work and returning home by the same means.

During the 2nd World War, Kernick was in the Royal Army Service Corps as a driver delivering supplies to the front line. He saw action on "D" day and helped to relieve the concentration camps, a memory that was to stay with him for the rest of his life, so much so that his first visit to Truro crematorium was particularly painful.

Joan recalled that he worked for two Perranporth builders, Godfrey Thomas and Plimley, and helped to build the council houses at Mithian and the clock on the inner green at Perranporth.

Kernick was involved in local community life through his membership of Mithian Men's Institute and his stewardship at Mithian Wesleyan Chapel. He was also proud to be Chief Marshall for the West of England Traction Engine Society at its annual rally.

During the 1st World War his father, Wm Eley, drove a steam engine delivering loads of explosives from Noble's factory on Perranporth aerodrome to Hayle. Joan's husband, Ralph (Uglow) said that the Mithian Downs road was unsurfaced and very rough in those days due to the regular usage by the steam engines. Spar stone would be dumped in the ditches so that the roads could be made up as and when necessary.

In the 1950s, Kernick found a Stone Age axe on the farm and in 1956 he donated it to the County Museum at Truro.

Kernick had a great sense of humour and a love of everything Cornish. He would delight in using an old local phrase that no one else knew. For instance, he once asked me, "which side is London?" Meaning, which side of this wall is to be the best side. Another of his favourites relating to an untidy building site, was, "Tis like Lansun jail here." His humour could be described as "dry" or ironic as typified by his statement when fighting in the Ardennes. Lying in a shallow trench full of water with bullets flying all around he looked at his mate and said, "We may be enjoying this now but we'll suffer for it in later life."

Ken Miners was born in 1927 at Penwartha and moved to Goshen Farm, Mithian at the age of two. He had a twin brother, Roy, who farmed at St. Agnes and who died in 2002.

Ken's boyhood recollections of the 1930s are many and include not being allowed in the Pub and attending Sunday school and Chapel on Sundays. His mother, Frederica, was in the Chapel Choir and Ken continued the association by becoming a trustee. Pocket money had to be earned and usually came from catching rabbits and selling them to Tonkins of King Street Truro on the way to school.

Apart from his father's farm at Goshen, Ken rented 16 acres at Silverwell and in 1943, at the age of 16, he bought his first livestock from a farm in Summercourt. They were six North Devon Ruby Red steers that he raised for beef. The next lot were four 18-month old South Devons that he bought from Noel Hoskins for £54 each. He was told that he had paid too much for them but as he said, "They gave me a profit."

Ken remembers buying his first car in the late 1940s for £70. It was a 1936 black Austin 7 Ruby, registration number DXN 67. He said that it couldn't have been too bad as Roy borrowed it to go on honeymoon.

In 1954, Ken's father, Harry Miners, died and Ken took over the farm. A year later, Ken married Betty (she said that they must have met in the dark) and they had one daughter, Janice. They farmed at Goshen until 1990 when they moved to a new bungalow, Rose Meadow, Mithian, where they still live.

Betty, née Pearce, was from Lambriggan, Penhallow, and she attended Penhallow School. Ken attended Mithian School up to the age of eleven when he transferred to Truro.

Ken's contemporaries were many of the people mentioned elsewhere in this book, Arthur & Ken Benney, Ronnie Symmons, Rex Williams, Courtney and Sylvia Jenkin. He and Betty have proved invaluable as a source of information for this book and I promise now to leave them in peace to enjoy the rest of their retirement.

Courtney Jenkin was born in Constantine in 1924 the son of William and Christine (Christian) Jenkin. He had an elder brother, Ronnie and a younger sister, Sylvia and in 1932 they moved to Mithian Farm which was a Cornwall County Council holding.

His father died in 1935 and his uncle, Thomas John Glasson worked the farm following his move from Carn Vellac Farm, which now lies beneath the waters of Stithians reservoir.

At the age of fourteen Courtney started work at Tresedder's Nurseries but he was one of ten people laid off just six months later when World War II started. He then found work on the Trevellas aerodrome where he and about forty other farmers, with their horses and carts, were employed picking up stones that were transported to Nanckuke for the construction of runways.

He recalls that life was tough in the 1930s and it was not uncommon for children to have shoes with large holes in them or even to share a pair and to attend school on alternate days. His mother had to carry water in large cast iron kettles from the yard to the Cornish range in her kitchen and he still has the old coppers (boilers) in which she did her washing.

He attended Mithian School until he was eleven years old when he transferred to St. Agnes School. He walked, each day, to St. Agnes, carrying with him, "A bit of bread and cheese or an occasional pasty for lunch."

Courtney started work on the family farm at fifteen and still lives there. In the early years all of the work was carried out using horses and he remembers their cob, "Major", who lived to the grand old age of thirty-five. The cob was replaced by a Suffolk Punch; also called, "Major." In the 1960s he became mechanised and bought a second hand Ferguson T20 tractor for £180 and he can still be seen driving it about the village.

He still has a 1938 McMichael, five-valve wireless that he bought from Harry Thomas of Trevellas, "But it needs a bit of work done on it."

William John (Jack) Roberts was born at Whitestreet on 17th September 1909, the only son of Edward John & Mary Elizabeth Roberts née Shackley. They lived at Whitestreet in one of the cottages near the now derelict chapel. He had two sisters, Phyllis and Jessie, and both are mentioned elsewhere in this book. His parents later moved to Higher Mithian Farm where they lived from about 1913 to the 1950s.

In 1935 Jack married Gwendoline Barkle who was also living in Whitestreet although she was a Camborne girl. They built their first home, a bungalow named Thornleigh, at Mithian Downs, where they lived when they were first married. Whilst there, they had two children, John in 1937 and Suzanne (Sue) who was born on Guy Fawkes night in 1946.

In 1949 the family moved to Treleaver Farm (Rose-in-Valley farm) which is now the home of John and Mary Thorley. They remained here for about six years. Although it was a mixed farm, they raised a lot of chickens supplying about a 100 a week to two Newquay hotels during the peak holiday season. Sue remembers helping to prepare the birds before she was old enough to start attending school. The day-old chicks were bought from Dick Pearce of Lambriggan (Betty Miners' brother) and were, "So cute that it seemed a shame that they had to grow up and be eaten." The run to Newquay in their old van (KRL 666), carrying the chickens together with eggs and vegetables, was made three times a week. The whole family were involved in the business and the children were expected to play their part. Sue remembers driving a Fordson Major tractor down a sloping field at Rose-in-Valley whilst her father threw out mangels to the animals. She could only have been seven or eight and she recalls having to press on the brake/clutch with both feet to slow the vehicle.

In 1955 the family moved to Wheal Davy Farm but son John died in June 1957 and the tragic loss brought to an end the plan that he would take over the farm.

Initially, Wheal Davy was without electricity and during the winter months milking had to be carried out by the light of, "Tilley" lamps. Buckets and milk churns were also in use as the large milk tanks of today were not then generally available.

Sue's memory of her father mostly involves him working on the farm, firstly at Rose-in-Valley and then at Wheal Davy.

Sue moved to, "The Orchard", in the centre of Mithian, in 1979 and currently lives there with her husband, Tony (that's me) and daughter, Louisa. Apart from the eight or nine years when she was first married, she has lived in Mithian all of her life.

Jack & Gwen moved to Shalimar, Mithian Downs in 1971 and lived there until their deaths; Gwen in 1986 and Jack in 1991. Shalimar is now the home of their Grandson, and Sue and Tony's son, Andrew Mansell and his wife, Hilary.

George and Muriel Symmons

The Symmons family moved to the village in 1932 to take over the grocer's shop. Mr. and Mrs. George William Symmons had four sons, George (B 1920), Ken (B 1922), Ronnie & Roy who, tragically, died at the age of fourteen. Ken moved to the village at the age of nine and attended St. Agnes School rather than Mithian; he says that it was to keep his elder brother, George, company.

George Jnr. commenced working in the shop at the age of fourteen. He remembers playing ping-pong at Trewartha Farm, "but there was always a price to be paid by carrying out some tasks on the farm." He married Muriel in 1948 and had a daughter, Wendy.

George and Muriel Symmons with their daughter, Wendy.

When they first married they lived at Perranporth in a chalet which is in the garden of the house where they now live. He and Muriel took over the shop from his father in 1950 and ran it until their retirement in 1986.

Arthur Benney was born on 3rd August 1928 **and Ken Benney** on 28th September 1929 at Trevellas Air Cottage. The family moved to The Terrace, Mithian, shortly after Ken's first birthday and a third son, Frank, was born there. Their parents were Percy Benney from St. Agnes and Ada Benney, née Burrows from Baldhu who died before Arthur reached his teens. After a few years Percy remarried, his new wife being Rebecca Jane Collins from Port Isaac.

Percy's father, Arthur and Ken's grandfather, was Richard Henry Benney who was a policeman at St. Agnes from 1896 to 1919 and he was the start of a four generation involvement with the force. His son Percy and Grandson Ken (1960 to 1973) became special constables and Great Grandson Clive, who was born at Goshen Farm Cottage, served full time and is currently a sergeant.

Arthur: - At the age of five, he earned 3d (1.25 new pence) a week from Jack James for taking his cows to Mill Pool each day. This was given to his mother who returned a halfpenny to him on Wednesday and Saturdays for sweets. As a 9 year old he took a job with Stanley Williams earning 6d (2.5 new pence) a week for working on the farm each evening after school, and on Saturdays.

When Jimmy Rowe took over Mithian farm, Arthur continued working there. He delivered milk before going to school at 9.00am and at the age of 11 he was earning 24/- per week of which he gave his father £1.00.

His first full time job was at Cligga mine where he spent just under 2 years working in the office and in the fitting shop. It was necessary for him to go underground on a couple of occasions and, in colourful language, he explained that he was none too keen on it. The mines were cutting back and he was made redundant and started a 12-year period of farming for Jimmy Thomas, firstly at Goonown and then at Hurling Burrow.

The winter of 1947 was very severe and Arthur recalls building a sleigh on which they took their milk churns to the pick up point. It was so severe that birds were frozen to death whilst seeking protection in hay bales.

It was impossible for undertakers to bury the dead due to the hardness of the ground and when this did improve it was still too treacherous to drive. He remembers one body being taken for burial on a Ferguson T20 tractor.

Anyone who has been involved in farming knows that the work is hard and the hours long but on one occasion he had to cut 5 acres of cereal before he started the 6.30am milking. He said, "I heard the larks waking up."

During the 1940s, when he was 17 or 18 years old, he commenced a seven-year involvement with the St. Agnes Ambulance Brigade based in Goonown.

He started his Greengrocery business on 12th February 1956 and recalls that the weather in his first winter was very bad. It was necessary to buy a set of wheel chains to keep his van moving and this was unbudgeted expenditure. Competition was fierce and he recalls there being eleven greengrocers in the St. Agnes area.

Life was very hard and busy as he was also farming eight acres of land and had acquired the old egg packing station.

Arthur married Brenda Jenkin of Scorrier in 1958 and moved to Higher Mithian Farm, Mithian Downs, where they had four children: Kevin, Andrew, Elise and Shirley. His greengrocery business was based here and when he retired in 1986 Roy Siedenburg took it over for a while. Arthur and Brenda moved to Trevaunance Road, St. Agnes and in 2001, to Threemilestone.

Ken – From the age of eight until he was about eighteen, Ken worked part time for Jack Chapman Snr. on his farm. His evenings and Saturdays were spent there for which he received 2/6 (12.5p) per week which he contributed to the family income. During this period he became proficient at tractor driving, ploughing and a variety of other farm activities. He also became very friendly with Maurice Chapman and they were such a familiar sight together that they were nicknamed Hen and Chick. Ken recalls that schools accepted that boys would be absent for two or three weeks in the year to help with harvesting etc but Jack Chapman was friendly with the Headmaster, Mr. Moore, and always seemed able to extend this a bit when there was a need. Apart from this official leave which Ken refers to as, "mooching off" from school he spent, "a lot of time working when he should have been learning."

He recalls that Mr. Moore boarded in the Miners Arms and another teacher, Mr. Houslop, lived in one of the Manor properties. Both of these teachers moved to Cornwall with the evacuees and Mr. Moore is remembered as a disciplinarian. He caned Ken on a number of occasions, but, having had enough of this, Ken called him a name that questioned his parentage, refused to bend over and got away with it. Oh, how I wish that I had had the courage to do likewise to a particularly sadistic teacher of mine.

At the age of eighteen he starting farm contracting on his own account but by 1956 the local farmers were beginning to equip themselves better and no longer had need of his services. He recalls cutting a field of hay for John Mitchell, at Trewartha Farm, before starting work "proper." This necessitated a 4.00am start but it had to be done. During the peak harvest period he only slept one night out of two, working continuously over two days and a night. In 1951 Ken married Mona and they moved to Goshen Farm Cottage where their children, Susan and Clive were born.

For the next few years he drove cattle lorries for Jack Chapman Jnr. before buying Beacon Farm which he worked for twenty-six years. Apart from the farm, Ken undertook a number of other jobs including sexton, bus driving for Chris Williams (1968 to 1973), maintenance work at Wheal Jane mine (1973 to 1978) and running his own cattle dealing business. Increasingly troubled by back problems Ken spent a great deal of time under treatment.

The picture was taken in 1990 and includes three generations of the Benney family: Ken and Mona Benney, Clive and Helen Benney. and their children Tom and Daniel (left).

At the time he was sexton all of the digging had to be carried out by hand and there was always the danger that the sides of the grave would fall in. To obviate this the earth sides were propped using long timbers called setts and these were held in place at each end by struts and wedges. Single graves were 6'0" deep, doubles were 8'0" and provision for three coffins meant that the pit had to be 10'6" deep. Considering the narrowness of graves it must have been quite an eerie feeling to look up at two walls of earth that could be quite unstable, particularly in wet conditions. Ken recalls being buried up to his thighs and having to call for help on one occasion whilst working in the Goonvrea cemetery at St. Agnes.

Since retiring in 1985, Ken and Mona have lived at Goonvrea Road, St. Agnes.

Beryl Newell was born on 15th October 1913 in Mithian and attended the local school from 1919 to 1927. She was the youngest daughter of Bessie and William Brown (Bill or Browny) and had two sisters, Mavis, born in 1909 and Hazel, born 1911.

The family lived in one of the cottages next to the Corn Mill; it is suggested that the three girls were born there, but number two River Cottages is best remembered as their home.

On leaving school she worked in service at Perranporth and Plymouth and in 1937, at St. Mary's Church, Truro, she married Merchant seaman Fred Newell. After a brief period when they lived at Trevellas, they moved into Sunny Villa, Mithian where their children, Peter and Angela (Angie) were born.

Her father, William Brown was a railway length man who worked on the construction of the Chacewater to Newquay line. He is featured in a number of places in this book and is appropriately shown as quite a character. Bessie was a local girl and was a sister to Geo Brewer Snr. Bill died in 1964, his wife, Bessie, having predeceased him by 15 years.

During the 2nd World War Beryl took in a number of evacuees and one family, Doris Bartlett and her two children, Keith and Richard, came to stay in February 1941 for just a couple of weeks but did not leave until 1944.

The picture shows from left to right – Mavis, Beryl and Hazel.

Beryl had a great sense of humour and many people outside of her immediate family knew her as,"Auntie Beryl." The ability to laugh at events must have been severely stretched on one occasion when she was attending Jack and Rona Chapman's wedding at Penzance. Heather Harvey remembers her being pregnant with Peter and wearing a flowing dress of very fine material. Her dress caught in the wedding car door as it drove away leaving her standing in the remaining top half of the dress and her petticoat. She is remembered for her generosity, her kindness and her eagerness to help others. The kettle was always on in her kitchen and her favourite expression was, "There is always room for one more." Her home was "open house" at Christmas and she did not like the thought of anyone being alone at that time of the year. Angie says that she remembers her Mum cooking for 20 people or more with most of the guests sitting with trays on their laps as there was not enough room at the table.

Beryl was a staunch member of the Mithian Women's Institute and was very proud to have been made an honorary member.

Beryl was widowed in 1975 and in 1987 she moved to St. Agnes where she lived until her death in 2002. Such was the affection for her that when she left Mithian she was presentated with a painting of Wheal Coates mine. She died after breaking her femur and contracting MRSA at Derriford Hospital.

Franklyn Ennor was born in Mithian in 1897 and was a familiar figure around the village until his death in 1991. There is some confusion regarding his actual birthplace and both Millpool and Magor's Mill have been suggested. Edna Evans is adamant that Franklyn told her that he was born in the now derelict Magor's Mill so we will settle for that.

He fought in the First World War spending a period of time in India. His future wife, Florrie, worked in an ammunition factory and, like many of the girls there, placed notes in the ammunition boxes for the, "boys" at the front to find. Franklyn found the note and, as they say, the rest is history.

Franklyn was involved in many aspects of village life and his name appears in many sections of this book. He loved brass bands, choirs, the Chapel and football (the round ball game). He organised many concerts involving the first two and played an active roll in chapel life and football.

He spent much of his working life helping out on local farms and is remembered as a particularly good hedger.

One of his pleasures was to smoke rolled tobacco in his pipe but he was not allowed to do so indoors. On dark winter evenings an eerie bright glow was often to be seen outside his house as he sucked on his pipe. Apart from his pipe, he was easily recognised by the dark brown trilby hat that he was rarely seen without. He drove a black Ford Anglia car and on Sundays he collected Bernice Kellow and took her to Chapel. He invariably had trouble in negotiating the entrance into the chapel grounds, managing to turn the wheel too soon and to slide down over the bank.

Franklyn & George Symmons Snr. won some money on Vernon's Pools. Franklyn built a bungalow on a style he had seen at Indian Queens and named it, "Aston Villa" (I think that that was the final required draw). Florrie's mother lived in the bungalow next door.

The Dymond family were gypsies who lived in tents, or more correctly under tarpaulins strung over a line, at Mithian Downs, during the

1930s. They camped at the entrance of the lane leading to Goverley and this location was used by other gypsy groups after they moved. Jim and his family later lived in the area near Wheal Liberty before moving into a disused gun turret on the aerodrome.

Jim and Kathryn Dymond had four children, Albert, Kathleen, Maurice and Stanley and in 1958 they were re-housed at Cameron Estate, St. Agnes.

Jim liked the occasional drink in the Miners Arms and even had his own chair by the fire. He was known to regularly fall asleep before he could get to his home, in a barn, cowshed or wherever. He earned his living by doing casual work on the local farms and his wife made and sold pegs.

The only time that there seemed to be any trouble was when other groups of gypsies came into the area and tried to set up camp on Jim's domain.

Maurice Chapman was born at Barkla Shop on the 19th January 1921 and died on the 2nd January 2003, just a few days before I was due to meet him regarding this book. He married Avril Megan Common of Roach on the 1st July 1944 and they had two sons, Roger (born in 1946) an Ian (born in 1949).

In 1957 the family moved from Barkla Shop to Mithian Farm Cottage where they farmed the 40 to 45 acres until 1975 when they returned to Barkla Shop to live in their newly built bungalow, "Demelza."

The photograph shows Maurice with his eldest son, Roger.

Avril had been working for the Mitchells at Trewartha Farm as a Land army girl in 1942 when she met Maurice at a whist drive in the Women's

Institute. They both enjoyed playing whist and often attended the many whist drives in the area.

His parents were William John (Jack) and Edith Chapman who were living in Tuckaway Thatch around the 1910s when their first two children, Ernie and Millicent, were born. The remainder of the children were born in Barkla Shop. Jack and a brother had returned home from Australia at the age of nine to the Callestick area.

On leaving school Roger worked for Reynolds the butchers at Perranporth and in 1965 the Chapman family bought the shop. Maurice continued with the farm but Ian became progressively more involved in the new family butcher's business. In due course the entire family were involved and it is now a thriving butcher's shop.

Maurice was a Parish Councillor during the 1960s to 1980s and was the Chairman on two occasions. He was a member of the Men's Institute and a Trustee of Mithian Chapel.

Maurice had seven brothers and sisters and the picture shows his parents and only seven children as Dulcie had not been born at this time. From left to right they are: Honor, Stanley, Douglas on his Father's lap, Millicent, Ernie, Maurice on his mother's lap and Thomas John (Jack).

Mithian Today

The physical features of the village may have evolved slowly but the people have moved with the times and, in that respect, the community is similar to many others in mid Cornwall. It is now much more difficult to find anyone who was born in the village, or indeed, within the boundaries of Cornwall. That is not a criticism, simply a fact and many people who have moved here have added colour and variety of thought to the community. In this respect Mithian is very different from even fifty years ago when most of the inhabitants would have been Cornish born.

The chapel is no longer central to village life indeed it no longer exists as a place of worship, and the distant St. Peter's Church is somewhat remote from the village community.

The growth in supermarkets and the provision of easy access has ensured that only the largest of village shops can survive and we are left with no such facilities.

The demise of the Men's Institute as a village organisation was because it was no longer needed, it belonged to a previous age when entertainment and pastimes were simpler.

The public house still exists and, for many, this is the focal point of the village and long may it be allowed to continue in its present form.

The village activities are many and varied and compare with anything that was undertaken in the past.

I hope that you have enjoyed reading the story of Mithian as much as I have enjoyed collecting and compiling the information into book form. It is, of course, a story without an end because events continue to take place and the village evolve. Changes happen that may or may not be to our liking but I believe that we live here because it is a delightful place to make a home and bring up our children. Let's all do our bit to ensure Mithian remains that way.

About three or four years ago a village photograph was taken outside the Miners Arms and I have reproduced it here by kind permission of the photographer, John Watton FRPS. It seems fitting to conclude the book with a picture of the entire village – well almost the entire village. Although it was taken on a pre-arranged date some of us, including the Mansell family, were absent on family holidays.

ALES FOOD
Miners Arms
FINE FOOD
Miners Arms
DINING ROOM
BEER GARDEN
FAMILIES WELCOME
REAL ALES

Some Family names appearing in the book

Adams	Gilbert	Parkinson
Allen	Gilham	Reid
Anderson	Gillett	Retallack
Andrew	Gilman	Penrose
Anstis	Glasson	Piper
Arthur	Godfrey	Price
Badden	Goodman	Proctoe
Bailey	Gray	Pugsley
Baker	Green	Quick
Bashforth	Gumbrell	Rand
Bassett	Guttridge	Read
Bartle	Harrall	Reynolds
Baylin	Harris	Rice
Bending	Harvey	Richards
Bennetts	Hewitt	Roberson
Benney	Hine	Roberts
Beringer	Hoblyn	Rogers
Biddick	Hocking	Roskilly
Biscombe	Holderness	Roskrow
Bones	Hooper	Rowe
Bonnar	Hope	Royle
Boundy	Hoskins	Russell
Bown	Horne	Sellix
Brewer	Hough	Siedenburg
Bricknell	Hudson	Sincock
Brokenshire	Hunt	Skewes
Brooke	Hussey	Skinner
Brown	Ichet	Smith
Butson	James	Snell
Campbell	Jenkin	Solomon
Caunter	Jennings	Solway
Chapman	Johns	Strike
Charnock	Jones	Swain
Chellew	Kellow	Symmons
Clarke	King	Tamblyn
Clemens	Knight	Targett
Chetwyn	Lavin	Teagle
Chitty	Law	Thomas

Colwill	Lee	Thorley
Cook	Leonard	Tippett
Crebo	Letcher	Tredinnick
Croucher	Lloyd	Tregelles
Crozier	Lobb	Tremewan
Curnow	Locke	Trenerry
Damsell	Lockett	Trew
Daniels	Lord	Thomas
Dark	Lovering	Toman
Davey	Luke	Tonkin
Day	Keep	Turner
Dibbs	Kemp	Uglow
Dodd	King	Valteris
Docking	Magor	Varcoe
Dores	Male	Vials
Drew	Mannell	Vincent
Drummer	Mansell	Vyvyan
Dyer	March	Walsh
Dymond	Martin	Ward
Eastlake	Matthews	Warren
Eddy	Miners	Watkins
Ellery	Mitchell	Whear
Ely	Mohun	White
Eley	Moore	Whitehead
Ennor	Mora	Whitford
Evans	Morris	Wilkins
Facey	Nail	Williams
Flanagan	Newell	Williamson
Ford	Nicholls	Wills
Fowler	Oates	Woodhouse
France	O'Leary	Woodward
Fynn	Osborne	Woolcock
Gaide	Ostler	Wynslade
Geake	Otway	Young

Acknowledgements

There are so many people who have contributed to this book that I find it impossible to list them all here. Their names are recorded in the text and to all of them I give my grateful thanks.

There are some people that I must mention as they have contributed so much to the finished article.

Clive Benney of St. Agnes who has provided me with photographs, guidance, answers to my many questions and has checked much of the historical data.

My good friend Alan Murton of Goonhavern for his encouragement and for proof reading and correcting any English mistakes wot I made.

Sue Mansell, my wife, for supporting me through this labour of love and who, I am sure, appreciated being told that she is now one of the oldest Mithian born residents!

The excellent staff of the Cornish Studies Library, the Courtney Library and the Cornwall County Records Office.

And finally, my long suffering friends who must feel that they have lived every word of this book. I promise to talk about something else in future.